WHY DOESN'T MY FUNNY BONE MAKE ME LAUGH?

WHY DOESN'T MY FUNNY BONE

MAKE ME LAUGH?

Sneezes, Hiccups, Butterflies,
and Other Funny Feelings
Explained

ALAN P. XENAKIS, M.D.

Villard Books
New York
1995

Library of Congress Catalog Card Number: 94-61635
ISBN: 0-679-75946-8

Manufactured in the United States of America on acid-free paper
9 8 7 6 5 4 3 2
First Paperback Edition

To Elizabeth and Nicholas, who bring my feelings to life every day and then give them special meaning

CONTENTS

PREFACE

Our body speaks to us every day. It gives us updates on our overall health and feedback on what we do and say. I call the conversations our body shares with us "funny feelings." We know them as "butterflies," "belches," "blushes" and much, much more! Funny feelings are often humorous and nearly always fascinating. Yet, as adults, we try to avoid their presence and rarely pay attention to their meaning. As we grow older, we get a *little* inhibited and a *lot* worried that messages coming from our body are predictors of oncoming disease. The truth is that most funny feelings are normal responses to our changing environment. We frequently avoid acknowledging our funny feelings because we don't know what's happening to us and are scared to ask. What we don't understand, we often dismiss or just deny. When we were children we had no such problem. What we didn't know, our curiosity said, "find out!" We not only relished each conversation our body shared with us, we also forced the dialogue to take place.

As toddlers, we'd twirl ourselves in a circle to bring on dizziness and then squeal with joy when we toppled over. We'd giggle with each hiccup, laugh after each burp, and howl when we passed gas! I remember as a little boy that goosebumps and hives were just a few of the many body messages that mesmerized my brain. I believed that being happy was the same as being healthy. As a physician communicator, I've adopted this philosophy as the positive principle behind all of my work.

Since graduating from medical school, I've learned an important caveat about the delivery of healthcare: We all want to learn about our body, but only if it's good news! We want to know more about ourselves and how we respond to the stimuli around us. The idea for writing this book, and others that will follow, actually comes from you. After more than a decade of answering your questions in the examining room, on national television, and radio, I feel you've supported my belief that combining medical information, trivia, and a sense of humor is not only desired, but is truly an essential prescription for today's anxiety and stress.

Some years ago, in response to my first syndicated radio program called "Health: Your Best Friend," a ten year old from Kansas City, Kansas, wrote, "Health is not my best friend! Johnny is!" I've always remembered receiving this youthful but prophetic phrase. A young boy reminded the young boy in me that effective communication requires reaching a meaningful place in a person's life. The simpler the message the better. I believe the ultimate communicator is our body. It's a master at getting to the point. It doesn't indulge in idle chatter. When our body speaks, we just need to listen.

Newton's laws of physics teach us that for every action there is an equal and opposite reaction. Our body follows this principle too. We yawn when another adult yawns. Yet, curiously we don't yawn when a child does. We itch-scratch-itch in a cycle that drives us crazy. How can we stop? Our skin shrivels up in water but every other material we know expands. Alcohol has less to do with hangovers than we think, in spite of what our stomach and head tell us! Pressure causes air bubbles in ponds and lakes to rise to the top (surface). Yet, even though our body is mostly water, there is another reason gas in our body sometimes travels to our top (mouth) and sometimes to our bottom. Even the sleepy seeds in our eye that we wipe away in the morning tell us whether they were caused by tears of sadness or tears of joy.

Today, white coats and stethoscopes mean only one thing to most of us . . . we've got a problem that needs fixing! This book will help you over that hurdle. When you're finished reading, your childhood curiosity for learning about your body will return. You'll talk about your body's funny feelings at parties and social gatherings. You'll enjoy having conversational health trivia at your fingertips instead of depending on the same depressing diet of medical war stories that everyone else uses.

Do yourself a favor: Unlike other books that you read and put away, place this one out on your coffee table, bedroom night table, or bathroom reading shelf. Each funny feeling can be read and referenced whenever you want to interpret a heart-to-heart talk with your body. Don't be frightened that some obscure disease is lurking behind every hiccup or hive we have. Remember, our body never stops speaking to us. Choosing to ignore a good conversation with our body about a funny feeling is simply robbing ourselves of some of the best and most entertaining conversation we'll ever know.

Have fun with my book, but please, don't use it for diagnostic or instructive purposes. If you feel concerned about a funny feeling you're having, contact a doctor immediately.

ACKNOWLEDGMENTS

Ever since I was a child, my parents have instilled in me the idea that the process of going through life is as important as attaining a goal. A very significant part of the process is the team that gives you support and guidance along the way. I can vividly remember bringing my report card home from school. My dad would immediately look at the side that held the grade on how well I worked with others. It was the only "A" I truly needed to earn.

Hopefully, this book is a reflection of what my dad taught me. I trust you will enjoy reading *Why Doesn't My Funny Bone Make Me Laugh?* as much as I enjoyed writing it. However, in terms of achievement, the evaluation is already in on the people who have given me their support. Each person has gained top honors in my report card. I thank them all with deep admiration and gratitude.

Thank you to Central Catholic High School and Warren Hayes for introducing me to writing and enjoying the art of communication.

To my teachers Richard Egdahl, Ruth Levine, and Mark Moskowitz at Boston University School of Medicine, who supported my belief in using fundamental knowledge in a creative way to reach an audience, rather than a tired and sterile approach.

To my brothers Randy and Mark, my sister, Pam, and their families, and to my mom and dad, I say, "Thank you for being yourselves."

To my trusted business partner and close personal friend, Chris Jenny, for his continuing support and encouragement.

To my good friends Louis Marx, Bill Bennett, Earl Greenburg, Don Pascal, Craig Najjar, Dave Caruso, Bill Wiseman, Whitney Clayton, Rich Boudreau, Michael Early, Ed Bergeron, Bill Curtin, and Sid Gorovitz—thank you for your support whenever and wherever it was needed.

To my special professional colleagues and associates Josh Shapiro, Steve Smith, Laurie Donnelly, Rennie Shepen, Peter Casey, Joe Doyon, Lois Lindauer, Bob Roche, Julie Wood, Diane Robinson, Bob Chandler, and Dave McKenzie—thank you for your listening ears, critical eyes, and total understanding.

To my colleagues in radio and television, Nancy Snyderman, Paula Zahn, Art Ulene, Tim Johnson, Curt Gowdy, Kate Sullivan, Larry Glick, and Ernie Anastas—thank you for your dedication and professional spirit to the art of communication.

To Kim Cotter for her assistance in research, Debbie Adams for her help on the manuscript, and Amelia Sheldon for her total coordination of this project—thank you for making this book a reality.

To Marvin Glass, whose illustrations have added just the right amount of fun and whimsy to these pages.

To my agent, Jeff Herman, who believed in this project from the beginning, my grateful thanks.

To my editor, Emily Bestler, for her support, intuition, patience, insight, and most of all, for embracing me as a writer and communicator. Emily's focused editing and sensitivity to my vision kept the spirit of this book on course throughout its evolution. I was truly blessed with a superb editor.

To my wife, Elizabeth, who encouraged me to complete this project despite the sacrifices to our relationship.

And to my son, Nicholas—never has a father so cherished such a loving child. I thank you for showing me how to dream and then how to live that dream in simple ways.

WHY DOESN'T MY FUNNY BONE MAKE ME LAUGH?

BELCHING

We eructate several times a day. I bet you're saying, "How can I eructate? I can barely pronounce the word." Well, depending on the social circles in which we travel, we're either appreciated for our courteous indulgence or we're chided for our rude behavior. Either way, eructation is the medical euphemism for burping or belching.

If we travel to a Middle Eastern country, a well-timed, hearty belch signifies our pleasure to the host for serving us a fine meal. The reverse is often true in other cultures. In Western society for instance, the only well-placed belch is a silent one. That's a belch that occurs far from any listening ears that would find the action offensive. A silent belch is actually an oxymoron since belching, by definition, is burping that is accompanied by sound.

Many of you probably have wondered where the gas that we normally "burp up" (versus flatulence, which is "burping down") comes from. There are two main sources. We either swallow air directly into our stomach, an event called aerophagia, or we produce gas through bacterial and chemical reactions in our stomach and intestines.

In addition to breathing air into our lungs, we normally swallow and dissolve about one liter of air per hour into our stomach. A liter of air is equivalent to the volume of gas in an average size party balloon. Anxiety and excitement, however, dramatically increase our tendency to swallow air. A good fright or a real stressful time can deliver more than five balloons worth of air to our stomach in an hour. Since our body cannot quickly dissolve this amount of gas, we usually burp or belch to seek relief from the discomfort and distension that results.

Although anxiety is common to all of us, the second leading cause of the air swallowing that precedes a good belch may surprise you. If you guessed chewing gum, you're right. When we chew gum, we create excessive saliva in our mouth. Our constant effort to swallow this saliva causes us to gulp extra air. Approximately ten minutes of gum chewing gives the tummy all the air it needs to issue a respectable belch.

Of course, not all air gulping is unconscious. Much to the chagrin of parents and teachers, thousands of children and teens gulp large quantities of air. Their game is usually to get attention by producing the loudest belch or the longest series of belches possible. Many adults, aside from the anxiety-provoked reflexive air swallowing already mentioned, swallow air intentionally in response to stress. Intentional air swallowing is a way of demonstrating some form of primitive control in an otherwise stressful situation. Subsequent belching is thus a conscious form of seeking relief.

Although nearly three quarters of our belches come from swallowing air (a rule of thumb is that excessive stomach air results in belching and excessive intestinal air brings on flatulence), we make gas in our bodies, too. Our normal body bacteria actively breaks down the food we eat. Meals high in carbohydrates (pasta and sugar) and amino acids (baked beans) produce hydrogen gas. If we have a lactose intolerance, our belches are made of hydrogen gas as well. A brief recollection of the Hindenberg blimp experience reminds us, that unlike air-swallowing belches, bacteria-produced hydrogen gas belches are highly flammable.

No explanation of the causes of belching is complete without mention of fiber, carbonated beverages and bicarbonated antacids. Individually, each of these foodstuffs causes hydrogen and carbon dioxide (carbonate) gas to accumulate in our stomach and intestines. Although they're responsible more for flatulence then belching, a good belch often occurs about thirty minutes after having eaten. If we start our day with a high grain and fruit breakfast, drink several glasses of carbonated soda as the morning drags on, or take several antacids to meet the stress challenges of the day, chances are eructating will become quite a familiar word after all.

THE BENDS

Most of our exposure to the "bends" (decompression sickness) comes from what we've seen on television or at the movies. A typical bends scene depicts a diver frantically ascending from the bowels of the ocean trying desperately to escape a finned killer. His escape usually ends with him being taken on board his ship, doubled over and writhing in pain. We're watching a diver who isn't suffering from fright but rather from the formation of nitrogen gas bubbles in his blood and body tissues. These bubbles are the result of his rapid movement through decreasing levels of surrounding pressure.

The bends got its name in the mid-1800s from men who worked in "caissons" or watertight boxes while doing underwater construction work on the foundation of the Brooklyn bridge. At the conclusion of each shift when the workers left their pressurized caissons, they developed pain in their joints. The workers described the pain as similar to "something boring into their bones." The workers often twisted and turned into the Grecian Bend in an attempt to relieve the pain they felt. The Grecian Bend was so named because people assumed the posture by sucking in their stomachs and pushing out their chests, and in doing so their bodies took the shape of a Grecian urn. Unfortunately, like the contortions that we make when we have a full bladder, the Grecian Bend provides minimal relief to the suffering diver.

What exactly causes the bends? When we dive or work in a compressed-air environment, we breathe air under conditions of greater than ambient or standard pressure. This increased pressure causes us to inhale larger amounts of oxygen and nitrogen gas than we normally do. These gasses are directly deposited into our blood and tissues. As we work, we use up the extra oxygen, but the extra nitrogen is not used by our body and must be eliminated over time by our lungs. In simple terms, our body, which is primarily liquid, contains inert dissolved nitrogen gas in proportion to the surrounding pressure. When we are at surface pressure, our body contains as much nitrogen as it can hold and is said to be saturated. When we dive into depths of greater pressure, our saturation point rises and more nitrogen gas is driven into our body tissues and blood plasma.

The bends problem develops when a diver's ascent to the surface is not gradual. The nitrogen gas will try to equalize with the outside pressure too rapidly.

Theoretically, if the depressurizing were done slowly enough, the nitrogen would be released in proportion to the surrounding pressure and there would be no problem. Since it is not easy to do this, divers usually enter a pressurized diving bell that is brought to the surface and then slowly decompressed. The slow decompression allows the divers to exhale the accumulated nitrogen gas.

If a person rises to the surface too quickly and begins to have symptoms of the bends, gradual decompression will reverse the process.

In the early 1900s studies were conducted that formed the basis for the dive tables used by the U.S. navy to determine how much decompression time is needed for a particular depth. For example, a dive to one hundred feet would need forty minutes of decompression to prevent the bends. More recent studies have revealed that these dive tables are not foolproof. There are many factors that could make some people still susceptible to decompression sickness even if they follow the tables to the minute.

Those at highest risk of the bends are individuals who are overweight. The amount of fat tissue is an important factor to consider, because fat will hold a high amount of dissolved nitrogen after a dive. Individuals with high body fat might want to seriously evaluate the added risks of diving before attempting the sport.

Commercial divers, like those who repair oil rigs, can dive to depths of twelve thousand feet. Since they are paid by the hour, their employers often economize on the amazing amount of time it would take for them to slowly depressurize. They are kept in a saturated condition by staying in a pressurized chamber, and they are taxied to the job in a diving bell. A saturation diver will often go as many as twenty days with no direct contact with the outside world. Although the pay is reasonably good, this would not be the ideal job for a claustrophobic.

BLOATING

A very good visual description of bloating comes not from a medical text but rather from one of the greatest children's stories ever filmed, "Willy Wonka and the Chocolate Factory." This classic tale portrays a young character, Violet Beauregard, who is spoiled beyond belief. Winning the prized golden entry ticket and being given an "everlasting gobstopper" is not enough for Violet; she is greedy and wants more. During her tour of the chocolate factory she sees a piece of experimental chewing gum that catches her fancy. It contains the savory flavors of a full meal, including dessert. She can't resist sampling the gum, and she does so in spite of Willy Wonka's warnings. With every chew, Violet not only tastes the meal but experiences immediate side effects as well. She literally takes on the shape and color of the gum's blueberry dessert. Her body becomes distended like a wine barrel and her flesh turns blueberry blue. "It's the juice that does it," says Wonka. "Take her to the juicing room at once to be squeezed before she explodes."

Although many of us relate bloating to air or gas distensions, as in the proverbial "old bloat" who blows off hot air, bloating is more closely defined as retaining unnecessary fluid. If fluid is the key, then how much water does it take before our tummies show signs of bloating? One glass? Two glasses? How much? The correct response is much more! It takes nearly 3 liters of liquid before

bloating becomes evident (about the same amount of fluid we pass in our urine in two days). The reason we need so much water to show signs of bloating is due to the structure of our anatomy. About two thirds of the fluid we drink enters directly into our body's cells (intracellular fluid). The rest of the fluid becomes trapped outside our cells (extracellular fluid) and, when there's an excess, is responsible for our bloated appearance. Although unrelated to the cause of bloating, the presence of intracellular fluid holds the answer to the burning thirty- or forty-something question, "Why, when we haven't eaten any food or drank any fluid all day, can we still pass water?" The answer is that our cells, when not in the presence of excess extracellular fluid (bloated condition), releases about one third of a liter of water a day back into our body. It's this new extracellular water that unexpectedly fills our bladder and also causes the unfed infant to still wet his/her diaper.

As you might suspect, all our excess water is not voided. So under what normal circumstances do we retain more water than we need? For women, hormones play an active role in abdominal distension during premenstrual and ovulating times of the month. On average, three pounds of excess weight suddenly appears during this period and, just as dependably, disappears several days later. There is some evidence that men follow suit with a monthly body rhythm cycle that affects water retention, but the resulting bloating is much less, only about one pint of liquid.

For both sexes, water and salt play a crucial role in regulating the bloating process. One might say that water and salt "go steady" with one another. Our extracellular fluid volume is directly influenced by the total amount of sodium (salt) we eat and drink and is balanced by the amount of sodium our kidneys excrete. A large sodium load, such as the amount in a margarita with a salted brim or in a plentiful ham meal, will cause nearly three liters of body water to be conserved. This bloating is more than three to four times the weight of our salted treats and is enough to begin to cause our rings and belts to feel tight.

Some of you are probably saying, Wait a minute! How can a margarita cause us to bloat! Doesn't the natural diuretic effect of alcohol, causing us to pass water, cancel out the salt's effect of conserving water? The answer is yes and no. Initially, the alcohol will allow us to eliminate fluid at a faster rate than the salt. If we drink other nonalcoholic fluids before the excess salt is completely unloaded, we'll have a tendency to retain this new fluid.

The comforting news is that as long as our body is healthy, the normal clearing process of excess water through our kidneys takes approximately twelve to twenty-four hours. This is usually an acceptable enough time for us to recuperate so that, unlike Violet, being "squeezed" is unnecessary.

BLINKING

In bygone days, batting the eyes was considered one of the more important feminine wiles. It indicated a woman was interested but not so interested as to seem improper. While the art of eye batting required skill, concentration, and the right kind of eyelashes, blinking can be mastered by anyone. In fact, it is impossible not to blink.

Blinking is the body's involuntary protective mechanism for the eye. A blink takes less than a tenth of a second and occurs on the average of every ten seconds. The eyelid, which is a thin skin reinforced with tough fibers similar to cartilage, helps protect the eye from injury and keep it lubricated.

The insides of the upper and lower eyelids have a thin layer called the conjunctiva, a transparent membrane that acts like a windshield wiper by spreading tears over the surface of the eye. The lubrication enables the eye to move freely in its socket and washes out impurities. At least a tenth of the eye is exposed directly to the atmosphere. Without the constant cleansing blinking provides, the eye would soon be damaged and unable to function.

In addition to the blink reflex, as a defense against injury the eyelids will also snap shut due to loud noises or startling movements.

Involuntary blinking reflects our thoughts and emotional states. As the eyes are the "windows to the soul," the eyelids are indicators of how we really feel about things. Researchers have examined how blinking is connected to anxiety. The results have shown that people under stress blink much more often than people who are relaxed.

An often-cited example of this theory is an examination of Richard Nixon's blinks on August 22, 1973, during his first television press conference in the six months since the Watergate investigation had begun. Although his face looked calm, his eyes were practically a blur, averaging from thirty to forty blinks per minute. The average number of blinks per minute in people who have nothing to hide is fifteen.

This may have no practical application for the average person trying to determine if their spouse is telling the truth. So far no one has tried to claim excessive blinking as grounds for divorce. However, it is true that in some professions blinking rates provide useful information. Dentists can determine levels of pain by tracking blinks (although I would suggest that screaming levels are equally useful indicators). Psychologists use blinking rates to determine their patient's emotional states. As the study of blinking becomes more sophisticated it is being added as a category in medical histories. Irregular eyeblinking may also be helpful in diagnosing such conditions as schizophrenia and Parkinson's disease.

BLUSHING

Along with thumbs, blushing is one of the few physical traits that separate humans from the rest of the animal kingdom. We may be tempted to point to the changeability of our facial hue as yet another indication of our superiority as a species. It's more likely, however, that blushing, like a visible conscience, is nature's way of keeping us honest.

Blushing is a circulatory phenomenon. Although it has many triggering mechanisms, such as getting caught in a lie, meeting someone for the first time, discovering an open zipper or some spinach hanging from your teeth, it's true cause is the dilation of the tiny blood vessels close to the surface of the skin, called capillaries. The increased amount of blood then causes your skin to glow red.

Certain circumstances will cause blushing, but it is the hypothalamus, nature's temperature regulator at the base of the brain, that is the real culprit here. When the body experiences stress brought on by such things as a major embarrassment or unrequited lust, it responds by triggering an involuntary circulatory reaction.

The body pools the blood supply to the brain and essentially shuts down. When the hypothalamus perceives a higher internal temperature, it will respond by trying to release heat in a very quick way. This is an attempt to keep everything balanced and regulated. Your hands and feet will heat up, but since the face has the most fragile capillaries, the heat finds its quickest and least resistant escape route there. The result is a quick change in color: a blush.

Whether or not you will easily blush has a lot to do with the genes your parents have given you. Some people are more sensitive than others. No matter the color of their skin, all humans blush. For redheads the blushing is usually more visible because of their fair skin tone. But black people blush just the same.

Telling a lie will often cause you to blush. However, even though you didn't hear this from me, if you sip cold water while spinning your tangled web of deceit, you will fool your hypothalamus into responding only to the temperature change in your mouth. In other words, you will head the blush off before it starts. This trick is also great for those of you who frequent singles bars or attend office parties. If you nurse a cold drink, you can keep your feelings of shyness or attraction from revealing themselves on your face.

However, do not drink alcohol if you want to prevent a blush or a flush. Alcohol absolutely wreaks havoc on your internal thermostat. Too much alcohol will also make you behave stupidly, which will really give you something to blush about.

Spicy food lovers seek out a good blush. Capsaicin, a natural ingredient in chili peppers, can make you cry and perspire and will turn your face red. When the capsaicin hits the tongue, the hypothalamus reacts quickly to cause you to lose heat and cool down the body. This evaporational cooling is why people in Mexico, which has a very hot climate, like to put chili peppers in almost everything edible.

One of the side effects of menopause is known as the "hot flash." When a woman reaches menopause, there is a physiological drop in estrogen levels, which ushers in fluctuating surges of intense temperature discomfort coupled with head and neck flushing. Estrogen supplements can relieve some of this by helping to regulate the internal thermostat.

Too much of the vitamin niacin has also been known to cause blushing. Niacin, vitamin B3, when taken in high levels causes a body rash called the niacin flush. People describe it as feeling like their skin is on fire. Niacin is useful in lowering cholesterol levels, but too much is more than the body can regulate effectively.

BODY ACHE

There is nothing that will make you "want your mommy" quicker than the aches associated with a cold or flu. As if the runny nose, chills, and fever weren't enough, body aches can make you feel like you have been fighting a war from the inside.

The truth is, body aches are the result of a battle being waged inside your bloodstream as your immune system tries to fight off an invading virus. When a virus enters the bloodstream, the body releases the compounds interferon, interleukin, and prostaglandins, which raise your temperature, change your metabolism, and increase blood flow wherever your body may need it. Even though science hasn't determined the exact function of these compounds, they have found the greatest amount of them in the body during the aching phase of an illness. Unlike fever, chills, and sweating, body aches do not seem to serve a direct function in the body's war against a virus. They may just be an unpleasant but unavoidable side effect of the body's attack.

Heat rubs will soothe body aches. When you put a ventilated rub on the surface of your skin, the body will let off heat, which causes evaporation and produces a cooling effect.

Body aches are caused by inflammation and irritation. Heat rubs will soothe symptoms but will not get rid of the underlying causes. An anti-inflammatory drug will help.

Aspirin and Tylenol are not equal when it comes to quelling body aches. Aspirin will get rid of pain with its analgesic qualities and will lower temperature with its antipyretic qualities, and will also serve as an anti-inflammatory agent. Acetaminophen, the active ingredient in such products as Tylenol, will only treat the symptoms of pain and increased temperature.

Epsom salts works well to relieve the symptoms of body ache by reducing the irritation caused by increased fluid or swelling, which pushes the internal tissues against each other. A simple experiment illustrates the underlying reason epsom salts work so well. If you could connect two beakers together with a hollow tube, filling one with plain water and one with salt water, you would find that the salt would eventually equal out between the two beakers.

The skin is a semipermeable membrane that acts as a filter and functions like the tube between the beakers. While not all the fluid will be released through the skin into the bath of epsom salts, a great deal will pass as the salt content of the two environments works toward an equilibrium. As fluid is removed from the body there is less pressure and therefore less irritation on the internal tissues. This provides much-needed relief.

BUTTERFLIES

I f you have ever been in an elementary school play or waited in the wings for your first-ever solo performance, you know those funny prickly feelings in the pit of your stomach called butterflies, also known as stage fright.

Although you may not believe it while you are suffering from them, butterflies are not life threatening. Since butterflies are neither fatal, terribly painful, nor glamorous, little research into their causes has been conducted. Some scientists presume they are part of the "flight or fight" response so vital to our primitive ancestors' survival. When we are faced with danger, our brains alert our adrenal glands to pump extra adrenaline into the bloodstream to prepare to either fight or run for our lives. Anyone who has ever been on stage would attest that the "run for your life" impulse assuredly is as strong and primitive as it was millions of years ago.

The stomach has several different reactions to certain external stressful stimuli. If you are facing a public-speaking engagement for which you believe you are ill equipped, unprepared, and basically out of your mind to try to pull off, you will feel the sensation we call "butterflies in your stomach." The on and off switching of the flow of adrenaline gives us this butterfly flurry of activity.

In contrast, you see a slasher movie and do not particularly enjoy the sight of severed body parts, you might find your stomach turning in revulsion, the sensation we call nausea. If you are facing an IRS audit you might find your stomach "tied in knots."

In each of these situations the body is responding to stimuli with secretions of differing levels of adrenaline and noradrenaline. The body is very specific in its response to certain emotional situations. Butterflies is just a lesser degree and varying frequency of the "tied in knots" adrenaline overload.

One Ohio scientist, who prefers not to be referred to as the stomach response expert, has conducted research with an electrogastrograph, the abdominal equivalent of the heart's electrocardiograph. The results showed that the subjects suffering from acute anxiety registered a higher level of stomach electricity than those who were calm and relaxed. Stomachs normally contract about three times a minute to churn food. The study showed that when the stomach is "tied in knots," the contractions are more frequent.

Some of the earliest research in this area was conducted in the late forties and is actually responsible for introducing the butterflies phenomenon into the public arena. Two researchers had an unusual opportunity to see firsthand how the stomach responds to emotional stimulation. Wolf and Wolff were able to see the inner workings of one of their patients, a soldier, who had a permanent opening from inside the stomach to the external skin. They observed marked physiological changes in stomach function during differing emotional disturbances.

When the patient was faced with an anxiety-producing situation, there was a reduction of acid output and a decrease of blood supply in the stomach and also a decrease in stomach movement. The media, in discussing Wolf and Wolff's findings, termed this phenomenon "butterflies in the stomach."

CHAPPED LIPS

ips. Two fleshy folds around the entrance to the mouth. They may seem paltry compared to the heart or lungs, but they actually perform some of the human body's most important jobs. Lips are made of a ring of muscle covered by a thin layer of skin. In between the muscle and skin is a mucous membrane that gives the lips their soft smooshy feeling.

Without lips food would probably fall right out of our mouths. We would not be able to make certain sounds and would certainly not be able to whistle. Without lips the Mona Lisa would lose her mysterious smile and faces would be virtually expressionless. Most important, without lips we would be unable to kiss, and millions of teenagers would have to find something else to do with their time.

Without lips mothers and fathers would lose the best way to check their child's head for fever. Lips have more temperature receptors than other parts of the body, and thinner skin. If we had to rely on our thick-skinned hands to check for fever, it would take twice as long. And with children or sick spouses, every second counts.

Like everything, lips do have their drawbacks. It may seem that lips have color like other parts of the skin, but in fact they have no melanin, the pigment that protects skin from the rays of the sun. Lips get their color from the thinness of the skin and the hundreds of capillaries, the tiny blood vessels connecting arteries to veins, that lie beneath it. So lips are very vulnerable to sunburn. Sunburnt lips are dry, scratchy, and painful. Because the lips are so sensitive, a small cut in the skin can be very painful.

Wind, dryness, and certain foods will make your lips chapped. Unfortunately, lips do not have oil glands like other parts of the body, so when moisture evaporates from them, they have no protection.

When your lips chap, the first thing you want to do is lick them. This only makes matters worse. The moisture you put on your lips with your tongue will evaporate, and they will get even more chapped than they were to begin with. You can protect your lips with balms and sunscreens, or by avoiding the sun, wind, and foods that tend to cause dehydration.

Even though they require special care, lips are truly worth keeping and can provide you with endless hours of pleasure for years to come.

CHEST PAIN

The interesting thing about chest pain is that the most common kind is in all likelihood caused by anxiety. Of course, this can become complicated if a person is having anxiety over the chest pain.

The fact that a pain in the chest is caused by anxiety does not make it any less painful. During World War II so many soldiers on the front lines were disabled by anxiety-caused chest pain that doctors created the diagnosis of "soldier's heart," or neurocirculatory asthenia.

Why your chest aches when you become anxious is almost totally related to contracture of your rib muscles. Sometimes known as Tietze's syndrome (no relation to the tsetse fly associated with sleeping sickness south of the Sahara) costochondritis, or chest wall pain occurs during anxiety because our rib muscles are forced to react to a simple physiologic supply and demand scenario. Here's what happens. Normally we subconsciously breathe about fourteen to sixteen times per minute. Under conditions of anxiety we may double that rate and take much shallower breaths—the familiar word is "pant." Shallow breaths mean less available oxygen to feed our rapidly working rib muscles. The end result consists of pain and tenderness around the cartilage that connects our ribs to our breastbone.

Don't worry if you find yourself in a doctor's office with chest pain and you hear the unsettling phrase "precordial catch." The term comes from the fact that the sharp chest pain you have often occurs under the left breast. Since your oxygen supply differs ever so slightly on the left side of the rib cage from the right side, chest pain symptoms will often occur right over the heart. Hence the term "precordial." "Catch" comes from a colloquialism that refers to the resemblance of the rib cage to a mitt that is trapping your transient pain.

Next to anxiety, the two most common causes of chest pain are related to colds and the heart. Between the two, a cold captures the first-place award for its frequency in association with chest pain. When it comes to coughs and colds, whether you have true pneumonia or an uncomplicated case of upper respiratory infection you'll probably hear the term "pleurisy." Pleurisy refers to an inflammation of the membranes surrounding the lungs caused by a viral or bacterial infection. Although this condition is temporary, unavoidable mechanical events such as coughing or even the simple act of breathing irritates the situation, precipitating the chest discomfort you feel. Cough drops and rest go a long way toward quickly relieving the symptoms.

While most people associate chest pain with heart disease, the fact is, heart disease is not the major cause of chest pain. Even the popularly believed heart attack syndrome of chest pain beginning over the heart and radiating to the left shoulder, arm, neck, and jaw rarely presents itself this way. While the majority of chest pain is musculoskeletal in origin and can usually be self-diagnosed as such when the chest pain becomes more uncomfortable with basic movement, you should always check it out when you are in doubt, because most cases of heart disease are treatable.

A quick tip: If every time you eat at a Chinese restaurant you find you have a burning sensation in the chest, arms, and legs and shortness of breath, do not run to the emergency room. Instead, the next time you eat Chinese, order yours without MSG (mono-sodium glutamate). Most people believe that MSG, a flavor en-hancer commonly found in Chinese food, is primarily associated with headaches and associate few other symptoms with the popular ingredient. In reality, MSG causes more chest discomfort than headaches.

COUGHING

oughing is explainable as an explosive expiration of air that allows us to clear our throat. Sometimes we can control our cough and sometimes we can't. Although this definition sounds accurate, it doesn't come close to answering some of the more frequently asked questions we have about coughing. How does a cough drop work? Why is it difficult to stop coughing once we start? Are all coughs the same? Why does just thinking about a cough put a tickle in our throat?

Although the cough is familiar to all of us, few know that it's a reflex that can develop from several different sites in our respiratory tract. The sound and pattern of our cough depends on where the coughing stimulus begins. A choking type of cough is the result of our larynx (voice box) becoming stimulated. The force of a choking cough comes from the air we already have in our lungs. On the other hand, a clearing cough for phlegm or other types of mucous that begins in our throat (trachea) is called a mucociliary cough. A mucociliary cough is usually preceded by our first taking in a small breath to help increase our expiratory force.

Our throat normally has a small amount of mucous lining its walls. Resident cells produce the mucous to keep our breathing tracts moist and poised to catch any dust that may enter our lungs. The mucous is usually of no consequence, because we unconsciously swallow it (it sounds awful but we don't even taste it!). However, in the presence of an infection, like a common cold, or an irritation, like breathing dust while emptying the vacuum, our throat produces more mucous than we can handle. Our coughing helps to eliminate this unwanted mucous. From past experience, we know that our cough can either be nonproductive, without phlegm, or productive, with phlegm. Just one unappetizing fact here: White mucous usually connotes minor irritation and yellow or green phlegm signifies infection. Don't feel queasy, that's it for mucous talk!

What's the most common cause of a cough? The overwhelming answer is stress! Most of us are surprised by this response. A stress cough outnumbers a common cold cough statistically more than fifty to one. Granted, in our lifetime we could have 750 different respiratory colds without getting the same one twice, but in contrast, stress strikes us nearly every hour of every day. When anxiety does hit us—whether from exams, paying bills, getting embarrassed, or thousands of other scenarios—there is one common factor: with each stressful situation, we intentionally clear our throat and produce a small cough or two. One exception to this quiet nervous cough is the psychogenic cough or the school phobia cough that occurs predominantly in older children and adolescents. It characteristically doesn't occur during sleep, it is usually explosive and spasmodic, and it occasionally sounds like a foghorn. The school phobia cough is best treated with TLC and, if that doesn't work, psychotherapy.

Why does smoking cause us to cough so much, especially nonsmokers who find themselves in the presence of side-stream smoke? First, an important distinction! We're talking about a smoker's cough, not chronic smoker's bronchitis that develops with an expectorating cough some ten to twelve years after smoking begins. Smoker's cough is defined as an irritating cough that occurs because the cilia, or fine moving hairs, in our respiratory tract are stopped dead in their tracks by cigarette smoke. Nearly 60 percent of us who inhale cigarette smoke and nearly 40 percent of us who are innocently in the presence of that same smoke will cough to accomplish the mucous-clearing task our paralyzed cilia are unable to do. This immobilization of our respiratory cilia is the primary reason that smokers and smoke-exposed patients have colds twice as long as their nonsmoking peers. Without the efficient cilia system working, infecting germs are left primarily untouched while a smoker's cough tries ineffectively to clear them away!

Have you ever wondered why once we start coughing it's very difficult to stop? Here's what happens. Our cough reflex usually has three fundamental phases. Once our respiratory tract is stimulated, the first phase finds our glottis (the space between our vocal cords) responding by opening widely. With this action, an additional amount of air gets sucked into our lungs. The second

phase involves our glottis closing, while simultaneously our diaphragm and rib muscles (intercostal muscles) actively contract, causing rising pressure to develop behind the now closed glottis. Predictably, the third phase finds this growing pressure forcing the glottis to reopen with a rapidly charging expiratory flow of air. The net result is the explosive discharge we call a cough. If we have gas in our bowel, this exploding force will coincidentally cause us to have flatulence or as my five-year-old says "do a padooski." In chain coughing these three phases form a vicious cycle. Each cough irritates. Each irritation stimulates the opening of our glottis. Each glottis opening causes air to flow into our lungs, and our reflexive muscle contraction perpetuates the coughing volley. The irony is, the more we cough, the more we irritate our throat and the more we stimulate the reflex. The chain is broken when we are able to break the irritation!

How do cough drops (antitussives) work? There are generally two categories of cough medications. One type is called a cough suppressant and the other a cough expectorant. When we have a dry cough, removing the stimulus—cold air, smoke, stress—that keeps triggering the reflex is the first response. If we find that the cough has already caused our throat to become irritated even after the stimulus has been removed, then a cough suppressant containing the narcotic codeine or the nonnarcotic dextromethorphan may help. These suppressants work by muting the nerves at the stimulus site and blocking the reflex cycle from reoccurring. It's important that suppressants be only taken for dry coughs; otherwise they may hinder our coughing up sputum and delay our recovery from a cold. If we do have a wet cough, then medications called expectorants are intended to help our productive cough loosen up the irritating mucous that's triggering the reflex. An anecdotal tip here: I have personally found that drinking plenty of fluids, using a humidifier, and sucking on hard candies are all equally effective in liquefying nasal and trachael mucous. In short, our expectations of a prescription or over-the-counter expectorant's capacity for relieving coughing discomfort are often too high. While we're talking about medication, here's a little-known pearl. For those of you who might be taking heart medication for high blood pressure called ACE inhibitors, be aware that, while the medication works well, for some it may cause a chronic cough. If you're in this category, you might want to have your doctor evaluate your situation.

One last question that's regularly asked is why does even the thought of coughing give me the urge to cough? People often confuse postnasal drip (PND) with this question. PND is not a psychological response but a constant water-faucet trickling type irritation that causes many of us to cough and clear our throats when we get up in the morning. The thought cough, however, occurs because when we think cough we also stimulate our salivary glands, which respond with an increasing salivary flow. This newly made saliva in the presence of our heightened awareness of a cough is often enough to tickle our throat and begin the coughing reflex.

A final word on coughing. Most coughs are our body's way of dealing with strange things that don't belong in our throat or lungs. The good news is that the majority of our coughs are normal and explainable, but if you have a persistent unexplained cough, see your doc—chances are you'll both be tickled that you did!

CRAVINGS

The word "craving" is almost automatically associated with the word chocolate. Anyone who has ever experienced a chocolate attack knows that nothing else will satisfy. You think about it, dream about it, and would give up just about anything for it. Is it all in your mind? Are you simply a compulsive chocoholic whose obsession will someday lead you into a size eighteen or Big and Tall shop? Take heart. You may indeed be compulsive, but that has little to do with your craving for chocolate. A craving for chocolate may be due to a lack of the brain chemical serotonin, which can leave you otherwise agitated and depressed. The lift you find after eating chocolate may be a direct result of the added serotonin that you have prescribed for your self with the purchase of that over-the-counter candy bar.

In general, people who lack serotonin often crave carbohydrates. It is quite possible that this chemical deficiency is at the root of obesity. If, for example, you crave chocolate, which is high in fat and slowly digested, you are going to have to eat a great deal of it before the brain receives the necessary signals.

If, when you crave carbohydrates, you satisfy the urge with sugary processed foods, you will create another problem for your already confused brain. Because they don't need to be broken down as much as other foods, refined sugar and processed foods immediately elevate the blood sugar level in your body. When the blood sugar fluctuates so rapidly because of a large influx of "empty" calories, you will continue to crave sugar in an effort to stabilize.

Cravings may be the body's way of staying in balance. Some researchers believe that whatever you crave is related to something your body might need to continue running efficiently. For example, if you crave salty things like peanuts and potato chips, your body may be experiencing fluctuating hormones, which affect its fluid levels. Sodium causes you to retain water, which in some situations may be necessary for continued good health.

Pregnant women are in a category all by themselves when it comes to cravings. I know one attorney whose only craving during her pregnancy was a shrimp dish at a particular Japanese restaurant. She would eat lunch there at least once a week and would go into an absolute depression if someone would have to cancel at the last minute. She joked that since she didn't like dining alone she would practically solicit strangers to go with her when the craving hit.

Actually, pregnant women have been shown to have changes in their taste perceptions. They most often like sweets or very salty things like pickles. The reason for this salt craving may be their need for water retention, since the body needs to increase water volume for the nourishment of the baby and the cushioning of the womb. Studies have shown that pregnant women who have severely limited their sodium intake have more complications in the later months of their pregnancies.

A craving almost as common as chocolate is ice cream. Ice cream is often thought of as a comfort food, because people often have a strong desire for it in times of stress. This might be a psychological effort to return to the simplicity of childhood. After all, who doesn't have great childhood memories of ice cream?

Even though the craving for ice cream is often emotional in origin it can also be caused by an overproduction of endorphins. When the body is under stress, the brain will produce endorphins, which allow the body to relax. The appetite for fatty foods is merely a side effect of endorphin production.

CRYING

Most of us think of crying as something a baby does. So let's talk about a baby's cry, but then let's look at our crying, too. Adults have occasion to cry every day but on average actually shed tears once a week.

To the untrained ear a baby's cry sounds like a noise designed to raise the hackles on the proverbial dead dog's neck. But a baby's cry is actually a sophisticated form of communication. There is a distinct cry that means "I'm hungry," a cry that means "I'm hurt," and still another that means "I'm cranky, wet, and stinky and want to go to sleep."

In actuality, babies do not develop tears until they are at least two weeks old. Their initial crying is usually a reflex action to remove particles or irritants from the eye (the corneal reflex that involves blinking and tearing that can also be activated by simply touching the eyelash). Reactive crying or emotional crying, which many pediatric psychologists believe is a learned response similar to adults, does not appear in babies until about the second to twelfth week of life. In either case, however, in about 5 percent of babies the tear duct fails to open, rendering crying with tears impossible. Fortunately, an opthalmologist can alternately probe and irrigate the offending tear ducts, frequently reversing this condition without an operation.

Wet diapers aside, both animals and humans normally have

three mechanisms for tearing: "basal or continuous tearing," "irritant tearing," and "emotional tearing." Basal or continuous tearing keeps the surface of the eye moist and helps prevent infection from airborne germs. Tears do not contain antibiotics, but their contents are interesting. The major ingredients of tears include electrolyte salts such as sodium, potassium, and chloride as well as water. Aside from water, one major ingredient is cellulose, the same basic substance you find in the vegetable celery. This cellulose is critical. It acts as a binder to hold the water in place while it keeps your eye lubricated. Another regular instance of cellulose, which moms and dads across the world have come to accept daily, might be more familiar to you. You guessed it. Cellulose is the major ingredient in the "sleepy seeds" young and old waking eyes have every morning.

Irritant tearing occurs only in the presence of a foreign object like dust or an elbow. When the surface of the cornea is irritated, the main gland of the lacrimal system (which includes the glands that produce tears and the ducts that carry them) reflexively produces clearing tears. Since the canals and ducts can only accommodate a set volume of tears, the overflow dribbles from the lacrimal lakes—the triangular spaces at the corners of our eyes—onto our face. Externally, this cascading process resembles emotional tearing.

Emotional tearing in response to physical or psychological stimuli is also accomplished through the lacrimal system. How we cry is easy. Some sixty glands produce tears, which ultimately either fall from our eye or are reabsorbed through our nose and throat. Why we tear emotionally is a little more complex. Our body's chemistry seems to play a major role in translating our stimulated emotional response to tears. The major crying center in the brain involves the pituitary and hypothalamus as well as the limbic system (yes, it is also the place where erotic drives are located). This network seems to work this way. Our learned behavior interprets a stimulus as upsetting or joyful. Reflexively, chemical neurotransmitters in the brain, frequently called in psychiatry "mood chemicals," are immediately released (norepinephrine, serotonin, and gamma-aminobutyric acid). These chemicals are regulated simultaneously in two major ways: First, a certain threshold needs to be reached for crying activation to occur—in other words, the strength of the stimuli is critical; second, the mood chemicals work through a negative feedback system loop. Simply speaking our brain normally uses the presence of mood chemicals "not to cry," so when a cry-evoking stimulus occurs, it creates a signal that actually blocks the mood chemicals in the limbic system whose function it is to keep us from crying. The result is that, until the blocking stimulus is removed, we will respond with tears. A practical application of this reflex action is that many antidepressive drugs work to unblock the activity of the mood transmitters so that depression and crying are effectively reversed.

A commonly asked question is, What determines whether tears are joyful or sad? The answer is that under a microscope happy and sad tears differ slightly. Sad tears appear to have a greater amount of cellulose and protein generated at a cellular level (sleepy seeds are larger and more common after a sad cry than a jubilant one). At a macro level our face and body language reflect a difference as well. Learned behavior tells the motor cortex portion of our brain when to switch on our facial muscles so that we might respond with a smile or an appropriate grimace. Simultaneously, mood chemicals "turn on" target cells in the limbic system, which respond with the suitable emotion of elation or depression.

The great "crying debate" over the centuries has focused on whether crying is to be discouraged as a sign of weakness or to be encouraged as an important and necessary catharsis for good health and well-being. Typically, men have been discouraged from crying, while women were considered "unwomanly" if they did not occasionally and appropriately shed a tear. In fact, in 1490, according to the antiwitchcraft book *Malleas Malficarum*, if a woman couldn't or didn't cry, she would be considered a witch.

Crying for both men and women has had cycles of historic acceptability in Western civilization. During periods of economic prosperity, such as the sixties and early eighties, there has been greater approval of emotional expression, but in times of economic downturn, like the Great Depression of the twenties or the recession of the nineties, emotionalism has been considered frivolous.

For babies, stimuli from A to Z can precipitate a good cry. But what about adults? Aside from the often-used phrase "don't cry over spilled milk," which covers a multitude of offending agents, are there predictable precipitating factors that conjure up a good cry for, with all due respect, "big babies"? An answer may be found through the work of William Frey, a Minnesota biochemist, who conducted the first widely accepted scientific study of adult crying in 1982. He concluded that women cry more often at interpersonal confrontations, while men are more likely to cry over personal reflections and "sad thoughts." The ancient Greeks probably said it best: "A good cry is good for the soul."

DIZZINESS

I n one of the great classic Greek myths, the treacherous sea
nymph Siren would lure mariners to her island with seduc-
tive singing. As the seamen approached the shore, knife-
like rocks hidden inches below the dark water's surface would cut
their ship to pieces. It was said that her adventurous call would put
the crew under such a "dizzying" spell that their actions were
uncontrollable and their total destruction inevitable.

In real life the good news is that most dizzy spells are not as
threatening as the ones Siren induced. They are normal, and each
of us averages about one episode per week. Although durations
vary, dizzy spells usually last from one to two minutes, and nearly
everything around us can stimulate an attack. For instance, look at
the basic difference in the sound of a chime, bell, and siren. Each
has a unique effect on our body. A true chime is harmonious and
makes us feel calm. A bell (not to be confused with the unsettling
effects of an alarm or gong) is melodious in timbre and brings out
our joy and happiness. A siren, however, alternates pressures of
compressed air in such an intense fashion that it will send many of
us into a state of dizzying anxiety.

Dizziness is usually a symptom and not an illness itself. The
causes of dizziness are rarely serious. In fact dizziness is often
related to periods of sheer joy and bliss. In the entertainment
world nearly 5 percent of the fans at any major rock concert suffer

symptoms of fainting and dizziness. This swoon factor actually helps determine the number of medics on call at any given gig.

Did you know that there are actually two types of dizziness? There's the simple version, when you are light-headed, dazed, and a little unsteady. Now if you add to this scenario the sensation of either yourself "spinning" or everything around you spinning, this "Alice in Wonderland" toppling feeling is a more severe case of dizziness called vertigo. Many of us misuse the term vertigo to mean a fear of heights. The true term for altitude anxiety is acrophobia. The mix-up is fair, however, since heights cause many of us to feel "topsy-turvy."

Whether we jump at the sound of a siren, swoon over a pop star, or have too little water in our system, our response is the same—we are dizzy. Simple dizziness is most commonly caused by emotion, fatigue, or dehydration. Our blood pressure reacts to these stressors with a harmless momentary fall. With this drop in pressure our blood carries less oxygen to our brain, and we feel light-headed. Fortunately, unless our dehydration is severe, compensatory mechanisms immediately kick in, and our blood flow is redirected to the brain from our stomach (that's why we feel queasy at the end of dizziness), causing our light-headedness to be short-lived.

Simple dizziness usually strikes without warning, especially when we rapidly change position. Have you ever wondered why when you quickly bend over to tie your shoe or when you rush to get out of a chair you've felt lightheaded and unsteady? Under these conditions most of us are experiencing another form of simple dizziness called postural hypotension. Although this is more common in our middle to late adulthood (aging makes our blood vessels less flexible), the sudden mechanics of movement cause our blood pressure to drop slightly, resulting in a temporary decrease of blood to our brain. If you take a few quick deep breaths you will usually clear up this mild light-headedness by giving your brain the quick shot of oxygen it needs.

Unlike simple dizziness, the second type of dizziness, vertigo, usually lasts for periods much longer than one to two minutes and characteristically involves our inner ear. Patients best describe the disorder as their world spinning so fast "they must hang on to avoid falling." The two most common causes of vertigo are labyrinthitis and Ménière's disease. Even though both disorders sound quite complicated, they are actually very simple to explain. Fluid-filled canals of our inner ear called labyrinths help us maintain our balance. This portion of the ear is called the vestibular system. Without the vestibular system we would never be able to judge whether we're upside down or right side up. This interconnected system of chambers and C-shaped canals is lined with sensory cells that detect motion and change in position of the fluid. The system works through movement of the fluid, which stimulates the sensory cells to trigger impulses to the brain. Anatomically, this network is comparable to

a carpenter's level balancing structural timbers on a worksite. Labyrinthitis occurs when the labyrinth becomes inflamed, usually due to infection. If you have labyrinthitis you are usually very sensitive to movement and more comfortable when you are very still. Once the infection clears or antihistamines are taken, the spinning you experience with this condition subsides.

Ménière's disorder is a degenerative disease of the ear that is associated with hearing loss and ringing of the ear. Although it is not life threatening, it can be unpleasant. Easily the most celebrated case of Ménière's disease was attributed to an accused murderess. The term "dizzy lizzy" was coined for Lizzie Borden. Lizzie was a Fall River, Massachusetts, native who was tried for the brutal murder of her parents and brother with "forty whacks" of an axe on August 4, 1892. In spite of her assumed guilt by many, Lizzie was acquitted. Many witnesses attributed her crazed behavior during the trial to her complaints that her ears were ringing and her head was spinning.

DOUBLE VISION

Your eyes are like cameras. The iris of the eye controls the amount of light that enters it. The lens focuses the light into a light-sensitive area, the retina, which "sees" images and generates corresponding neural impulses.

The eye transmits the impulses through the optic nerve to the brain. Like a camera, the lens of the eye will produce an upside-down image, which is slightly different in each eye. The brain will translate the image and interpret it as right side up and three-dimensional. The images are basically sorted and stored in the mind's memory and then instantaneously recalled. They can also be later recalled as vivid memories.

In order for the images to be clear, the two eyes must take basically the same "picture" at the same time. If the two eyes are not aligned, the image will be distorted.

Some people will have a misalignment of the eyes through a paralysis of their eye muscles. But more common, many people experience double vision through a misalignment of the eyes caused by extreme fatigue or too much alcohol. Alcohol directly affects the brain stem, which is what controls muscle movement. The alcohol-impaired brain stem will slow the muscle movement in the eyes, causing them to seem like they each have a mind of their own. If the muscles of the eyes do not work in unison, you will see blurred or double images.

DROOLING

As an adult when you think of drooling it usually conjures up one of two situations: either a demonstration of excessive pleasure in something or unbridled anticipation of something else. When it comes to food, both scenarios include the production of an overabundance of saliva as part of our bodily reaction to a present or promised taste treat. For babies, drooling is one of the things they do best. Between the ages of four to six months, while they are cutting their first set of teeth, babies can drool one hundredth of their body weight.

The cutting of teeth stimulates the production of saliva, but it is the underdeveloped motor skills of a baby that causes drooling. In adults, when saliva is produced, it is quickly swallowed unless there is a nervous disorder present such as Parkinson's disease or rabies that prevents this normal reflex.

Saliva may not be the most appetizing word in the dictionary, but it's made up of chemicals that are common in our body. For instance, sodium, potassium, calcium, and chloride are all present. Saliva also contains a digestive enzyme called amylase that begins breaking down carbohydrates in our mouth, unlike proteins and fats that are primarily broken down in our stomach and intestine. (This is why drooling occurs more frequently in relation to carbohydrate-laden meals than those heavy in fat or protein).

A frequently asked question that puzzles even the most inquis-

itive gourmet is, Why do we salivate when we think of something delectable and delicious? The answer may surprise you. We salivate when we taste food. Yet physiologically we taste food only when it begins to dissolve in our mouths. Since we need saliva to dissolve food, how does saliva become produced before tasting occurs? Sounds like the chicken and the egg story doesn't it? The trick is that pictorial and verbal cues play a critical role in producing saliva even before the food arrives in our mouths. In essence, the normal process of manufacturing saliva frequently begins, not with the mechanical presence of the food on our tongue as most would believe, but rather with our imagining a taste from the words we hear and the sights we see. No matter how delicious something is, taste arises from the four primary tastes: salt, sour, sweet, and bitter. From this simple formula comes the awesome reality that, in spite of the immense number of combinations arising from varying degrees of these four primary tastes, our ability to drool begins with the brain's capacity to memorize past dining experiences and extrapolate from them tens of thousands of possible taste combinations. With lightning speed the brain utilizes the more than ten thousand taste buds on our tongue to discern the taste of one part salt in four hundred, sourness in one part in 140,000, or bitterness in more than several million parts. It is remembrances of these incredibly fine culinary resolutions that set our salivary juices going and create the fertile ground for our imagination to release saliva on arousal.

I'm often asked, When do adults drool the most? The answer has nothing to do with eating and usually occurs when we are sleeping and our mouth is completely relaxed and unable to swallow reflexively. The corollary to this question is, When do adults drool the least? The answer is when they are nervous and their salivary glands temporarily shut down (dry mouth) or when they think of something unappetizing like brushing their teeth in the morning and drinking orange juice immediately after. In case you wonder, here's why the juice tastes bitter. Toothpaste contains a detergent that breaks down the phospholipids (fat-like) substances on our tongue's taste buds and leaves them temporarily raw or tasteless. Following this event the basic chemicals in the toothpaste such as chalk and formaldehyde can cause a bitter taste when they mix with the orange juice's citric and ascorbic acids.

DRY MOUTH

I love the commercials about "morning breath." If you have ever eaten garlic or some spicy food close to bedtime, you know that no matter how many times you brush your teeth or what kind of industrial strength mouthwash you use, it may be some time before you feel like kissing or getting cozy with anyone again.

But that is a different situation than having your run-of-the-mill morning mouth. The reason you tend to have bad breath in the morning is simply because there is a decreased flow of saliva when you sleep. This enables bacteria to grow and accumulate in the plaque of your teeth.

A dry mouth can sometimes even interfere with your sleep. If you go to sleep dehydrated, you might dream all night about finding something to drink. There is no evidence about whether or not drinking something in your dream will influence the flow of saliva, but you never know. I have been told that dreaming about finding a bathroom can have embarrassing consequences.

When you are nervous, you can have instant dry mouth, because when your body perceives it is under attack it will exhibit the "fight or flight" response. This sends the sympathetic nervous system into high gear, heightening all bodily activity.

The sympathetic nervous system has two chains of nerves, which run from the spinal cord to all the organs of the body. The nerve endings release the neurotransmitters epinephrine and norepinephrine into the tissues and stimulate the release of epinephrine from the adrenal glands into the bloodstream.

When all of the bodily systems are accelerated, the heartbeat is strengthened. Blood rushes to wherever the body perceives a need to protect its organs from the impending attack. When you feel nervous, the digestive system is essentially shut down through this chain of events, which stops the production of saliva.

A dry mouth may be unavoidable in stressful situations, but you can counteract its effects by replenishing your water supply, sucking on lozenges or chewing gum.

FAINTING

ainting is not a sign of psychological weakness, nor is it a gender phenomenon specific to women. It's a symptom of lowered blood flow to our brain. Also called syncope, fainting is a sudden, brief loss of consciousness due to a decreased presence of blood in our head.

Contrary to common belief, men and women faint in nearly equal numbers. Women seemed to have unjustly inherited the "fragile fainter" moniker during the Victorian period. The fashion rage of the day dictated that women have an hourglass figure with an extremely dainty waistline. With whalebone corsets, women successfully achieved the external image of this calculated gentility, but the corsets nearly strangulated the stomach, intestine, and lungs of their wearers.

This drastic restriction of oxygen to the brain caused women to faint rather regularly. Relief and consciousness were dependent on cutting the corset laces. Occasionally an overzealous "good Samaritan" would unwittingly break a whalebone during the frenetic process. If the high-tensioned bone sprung inward, a subsequent puncture of a vital organ often occurred earning the corset's well-deserved nickname, "death cage." Luckily, under circumstances other than a fashion fad or a pressing whalebone, fainting stimuli are predominantly predictable and preventable. Among the leading causes of fainting are hy-

perventilation, exertion, low blood sugar, pregnancy, and lack of movement.

Generally accepted medical advice dictates that we should wait at least an hour after eating a meal before going for a swim. This helps prevent the risk of cramps in the water. Did you know that waiting an hour is just as important to prevent fainting? Here's why.

Immediately after we eat, our blood begins to pool toward the center of our body to aid in digestion. When we exercise, the peripheral blood vessels (those in our arms and legs) expand or dilate so that our working muscles can access more oxygen. The combination of these bloodpooling-reflexes frequently causes anyone who begins postprandial (after eating) exercise too soon to lose consciousness momentarily.

As we have seen many times in both television dramas and the movies, stress and anxiety often can cause fainting. Why does this happen? Normally we "breathe in" oxygen and "breathe out" carbon dioxide. When we are anxious, our breathing rhythm accelerates, and we hyperventilate. This intense, rapid breathing leads to an excessive loss of carbon dioxide resulting in a shrinking (vasoconstriction) of the blood vessels in our brain. Hyperventilation syndrome often follows. Its symptoms are numbness around the mouth, fingers, and toes. Fainting usually follows soon after. Athletes often faint in gymnasiums and athletic clubs across America by practicing rapid breathing similar to that brought on by hyperventilating. This phenomenon is called weightlifters syncope, and it happens when an athlete increases the number of breaths he takes per minute to raise his oxygen load and maximize his muscle strength. This causes a compensatory decrease of blood to the brain. The simultaneous lifting of weights also pools blood in the arms. This combined peripheral blood pooling and increased ventilation often causes fainting, especially when the weightlifter decides to overdo the workout.

Simple fright, if severe enough, can also cause almost instantaneous fainting. Our body has genetically and biologically adapted itself to dilate most of our peripheral blood vessels within tenths of a second when we encounter a truly "wooly scare." This preparation for flight after a fright leaves our muscles fully oxygenated to run but is too much for our brain to handle; often it shuts down, and as a consequence, we have an immediate loss of consciousness.

A frequently used but greatly misunderstood medical term called vasovagal response is a major cause of fainting spells. A vasovagal-induced faint is usually brought on by the sight of blood, a syringe needle, or the anticipation of similar pain which you may have experienced while waiting in a dental chair to have a cavity filled without anesthetic. The reflex works this way. Our senses bring the stimulating information back to our brain. From learned behavior our autonomic nervous systems respond, through the vagus nerve, to prepare for battle against what our bodies perceive to be noxious agents. When this response is triggered, the body conserves its energy in as many ways as possible. Blood engorges our internal organs and is rationed to our brain. The outcome leaves us feeling weak, with a nauseous stomach and clammy skin. If the stimulus is strong enough, we faint. You can help prevent fainting if you lie down or put your head between your knees when you begin to feel queasy. These postures allow blood to flow back to your brain. Recovery is complete within minutes. A maneuver that is frequently used in the navy for a sailor who feels faint after getting an injection and who also feels too macho to lie down is to have him push the back of his head hard against the resistance of another person's hand. This maneuver causes blood to rush back to the brain and gives almost instant relief from the threat of a fainting spell.

Believe it or not, the vasovagal response has also played a significant role in modern telephone booth design. You've no doubt noticed that most of the enclosed three-foot-by-three-foot telephone booths are gone. You probably thought that the major reason for their disappearance was the increasing costs of upkeep due to vandalism and regular maintenance. Economics is only part of the reason; health is another. When we are inside a telephone booth, we are squeezed. Our body has little room to move. There's not even enough space for us to fall down, and that's the problem. The horizontal position the body assumes when we have fainted is key to our recovery and return to consciousness. In a telephone booth, the fainting victim cannot reach the reclining position that allows the blood to flow back into the brain and revive him. In short, the telephone booth, while a boon to privacy, is a liability to our health.

You might have heard about the man or woman who has fainted while urinating or coughing. How does this happen? Under conditions of strained urination, when one is trying to totally empty the bladder, or during a spell of intense coughing, called blue coughing, (when we force ourselves to clear our lungs with such strain we turn blue), there is an increase in pressure in our circulatory system, which limits the blood returning to our heart.

This decrease in blood to the heart means less blood pumped out by the heart to the brain. The lack of blood to the brain brings on a faint. The whole process of increased pressure to our chest causing a subsequent decrease in the flow of blood to our brain is called valsalva.

FATIGUE

If you are a parent of a newborn, you do not need an explanation of how fatigue feels. You know it is more than just feeling tired. Each time you wish you had a forklift to get your body up a flight of stairs, you dream of the days when two A.M. was a time of deep REM (Rapid Eye Movement) sleep and not middle-of-the-night feedings.

Or if you are a weekend warrior who likes to relive glory days of athletic prowess once or twice a year, you know what fatigue feels like. After a round of tennis or a good basketball game with all your balding buddies, you might spend the next day on your couch asking for help using the remote control.

Before Thomas Edison invented the lightbulb in 1879, human beings were adjusted to the natural rhythms of the sun. We were early to bed and early to rise. Now that we can mimic daylight at any time of day, we have all sorts of ways to fool the clock. We can work all night and watch movies at four A.M.

It seems we have much more control over time than ever before, but there is a catch. We may have more time to do the things we like to do, but most of us do not have the energy. In fact, fatigue is one of the most common complaints modern patients make to their physicians.

Although there are many explanations for the fatigue that is plaguing modern society, artificial light is partially to blame. Artificial light has an effect on our energy levels because our internal regulating mechanisms were built to be light sensitive. For example, when light hits the retina of the eye, the pineal gland at the base of the brain is stimulated to secrete melatonin, a hormone that determines how rested we feel, whether we have high immunity, and how well our memories work.

For most of us who are on some kind of regular schedule, our internal rhythms adjust to a "normal" asleep and awake cycle. But when we are on an irregular schedule such as shift work, we become so light sensitive that we need to be "tricked" to go to sleep at night. Bright lights that simulate morning sunlight at dawn and then dim in the evening help us to fall asleep with regularity. However, bright lights in the evening are too stimulating and keep us awake until we are too exhausted to care. That's why attending a night concert or athletic event with bright lights keeps us awake for hours.

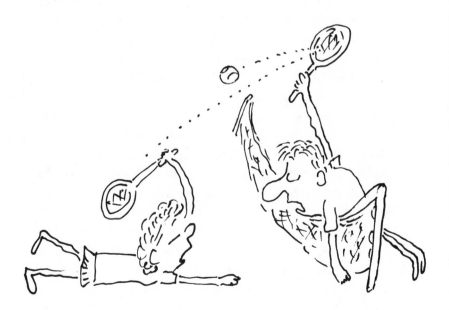

If you sleep with regularity you might still have two to four interrupted sleep cycles without even knowing it. If you live in a noisy neighborhood, you could be awakened several times each night without actually coming to full consciousness. Your lack of deep REM sleep will cause you to wake up in the morning feeling like you hardly slept at all.

If you have a nightcap to get yourself to sleep in order to avoid fatigue, the next day you may be surprised to know that it will have the opposite effect. The alcohol will suppress REM sleep and will then bring on a powerful surge of early morning REM. You are likely to spring awake at the wrong time and then spend those "dark hours before the dawn" cursing your clock.

If you keep your home temperature above seventy-five degrees, you will tend to wake more often and get less deep sleep than if you keep your home a bit cooler. If, however, you let your home temperature dip below fifty-four degrees, you are likely to have a restless night filled with highly emotional dreams. When you sleep, your body temperature automatically drops and your breathing slows, allowing you to sustain all body support systems while at rest. A room temperature lower than fifty-four degrees will make your body work too hard to keep everything in balance and will make you restless and out of sorts. Sixty-five degrees is best for a good night's sleep.

Your circadian system, the internal clock that influences your biological and psychological functions, plays an important role in whether or not you will feel fatigued. If you do something to throw off your regular body rhythm, you will either need time to readjust or will have to change your patterns to create a new rhythm.

People who frequently switch work shifts are likely to feel chronic fatigue unless they allow at least three days for their circadian rhythms to readjust. If you sleep in on the weekends you are likely to be happy but less energetic than if you keep to your regular schedule. Like changing a shift, even an hour difference in regular sleep patterns can throw off your internal clock.

Sometimes fatigue can be a signal that you are getting a cold or flu. It may be your body's way of telling you to slow down and conserve energy to fight the illness.

Nothing causes fatigue more than depression or repressed emotions. If you have no physical cause for your fatigue, you might want to examine how your life is going. People will often feel fatigue if there is something they cannot express. If you want to feel better, perhaps you should consider telling your spouse you can't stand him/her or telling your boss what he can do with his job. You might wind up divorced or fired, but you are bound to feel more energy.

FEELING HOT AND COLD

Many a marriage has been put to the test over differences in temperature tolerance. In fact, it seems likely that lawyers developed the concept of irreconcilable differences as grounds for divorce because of battles over the household thermostat. Well, this may not be exactly true, but it does illustrate the point.

All human beings have a unique way of responding to changes in outside temperatures. While most people have a stable internal temperature of 98.6, how we feel temperature is more a product of how our bodies produce or lose heat in response to our environment.

No matter what the external temperature is, our body will seek a thermal balance through all kinds of metabolic processes. There is an internal thermostat in the brain that keeps the body at its constant temperature. For multiple reasons, the body functions best at 98.6, so the brain has mechanisms to retain this balance.

The hypothalamus gland at the base of the brain is what monitors the temperature of the blood. It sends messages to the blood vessels to constrict or dilate according to how much blood needs to flow to the various parts of the body.

Your skin is what actually tells you if you are hot or cold. The normal skin temperature is eighty-six degrees, which is considerably cooler than your internal temperature.

If for some reason you are exercising to a videotape of Diet Workshop's "Lighten Up" and you become hot, your internal temperature will change. In order to keep a temperature balance your brain will tell the blood vessels in your skin to expand or dilate. This allows more blood to flow through the vessels carrying heat to the surface of your skin where it can escape. This will maintain your internal temperature, but you may still feel the sensation of heat.

If you are married to someone who insists on keeping the window open in the winter in spite of your claims of freezing to death, don't worry. Your blood vessels will shrink or constrict to reduce the blood flow to the surface of your body. This constriction will conserve the heat in your body to protect all of your vital organs. Of course you may also want to suggest to your spouse that he close the window or do something to protect his organs. A goose down comforter might be a good compromise to help reduce the chill you feel.

Although your body will find ways to keep your internal temperature in harmony with the outer environment, you may be more prone to hot or cold temperatures than other people because of many factors that affect the rate at which your body produces or loses heat.

For example, if you have a lot of body fat, you will tend to feel colder. Men tend to have less body fat than women, which is why it is sometimes useless for a woman to ask her husband if she needs to wear a coat outside. If he has been outside and she has not, logic would tell her that he should be able to give her this advice. However, although it might not be tactful, it is not a sign of total insensitivity for a husband to reply, "I don't know, see for yourself."

People are under the misconception that humans need more padding in the winter to keep warm. While body heat comes from food calories, becoming the reincarnation of Jabba the Hut will prevent the heat that is held in through vasoconstriction from reaching your skin. Your inner organs will still be insulated, but you will be cold.

Whether you are prone to hot or cold, there are ways you can adapt more comfortably to any environment. Five to ten percent of us normally feel hot. If you want to be able to keep cool, you might want to eat lightly. If you eat a heavy meal your body must work hard to digest the calories and this will make you feel warmer. A light meal has a cooling effect.

You should wear less clothing. You might feel conspicuous wearing short sleeves in the winter, but leaving your skin uncovered is the best way to create an escape route for surplus heat.

If you wear natural fibers that are absorbent instead of plastic or polyester, you will feel cooler, because moisture will evaporate.

To stay warm if you are a cool person, you should eat several times a day while remembering not to use this information as an excuse to create more body fat. Protein snacks will provide heat as the body works to digest them.

If you avoid stimulants, you will have less vasoconstriction, which will make you feel warmer.

Do not be fooled by alcohol. If it is very cold outside, a hot toddy will feel good to your innards, but you will be dilating your blood vessels. The increased flow of blood will produce the sensation of heat, but if it is really cold, the heat will not be reserved for your vital organs where it is needed the most. It is better to layer your clothing to give your skin the sensation of warmth while your body does what it can to maintain a healthy inner temperature.

FEVER

ever is our friend. When we have one we may think being hit by a truck would be preferable to the feeling of being burned up from the inside, but fever is a useful and important way for the body to fight against viruses and bacterial infections.

Fevers have many causes. In general they are the body's attempt to get rid of any potentially noxious intrusion. This means that we can raise a fever if we have too much sun, or even if we have a major blowout with our spouse. This is not necessarily our body's attempt to rid us of the noxious intrusion, but is a reaction to very intense emotions.

The normal internal temperature of the human body is 98.6 degrees. When you are ill, your body releases proteins called pyrogens at the same time the white blood cells fight against the invading microorganisms. The pyrogens influence the temperature-controlling center in the brain called the hypothalamus, causing it to raise the body temperature in order to help destroy the enemy.

No one knows exactly how a fever works to fight illness. It is commonly believed that an elevated internal temperature will stop the growth of bacteria. Another possibility is that fever makes all of the internal organs work faster. There is more of everything—hormones, enzymes, and blood cells—and everything works harder

to fight the illness. Our blood even circulates faster as our body destroys harmful germs. Although it may seem like you are burning up if you have a fever, most will not go higher than 106 degrees. If they do, the body will go into a state of hyperthermia, which can be fatal.

There is a great debate as to whether or not it is wise to artificially reduce a fever through medication. Some experts maintain it is best to let it run its course, because the fever will inhibit the growth of the disease-producing organisms.

Others feel it is beneficial to reduce the symptoms if at all possible. If you do not want to medicate but want to feel better, you can follow the example of the iguana. When an iguana gets a fever, its hypothalamus is reset to a higher temperature. But since the iguana can't generate enough internal heat to reach the new level, it must change its environment to suit its temperature needs.

You can reduce your symptoms by making your environment suit how your feel. If your fever causes the chills, you can crawl under a hot rock. It might be easier to stay in your bed with the covers pulled up under your chin, but this is strictly a matter of personal taste.

Contrary to popular folklore, you do not need to "starve a fever." Changes in the internal thermostat require the expenditure of a great deal of energy. So you need to eat to keep up your strength.

FULLNESS

You can't even discuss the subject of feeling full without thinking of the Alka-Seltzer commercial, "I can't believe I ate the whole thing." We've all eaten something that tasted so good that we couldn't stop. Like rebellious children we ignore the signals from our brain that scream, "No more! If you put in one more mouthful I'm going to burst."

The stomach is a large muscular organ that is shaped somewhat like a hotdog when it is empty of food. As food is chewed and sent to the stomach, it expands to look almost like a football, or in the case of the man in the Alka-Seltzer commercial, a beachball. Food takes about three to six hours to digest in the stomach, where it is converted to a soupy liquid called chyme. The liquid is moved out of the stomach by small contractions until it winds up in the small intestine. When the food is in the duodenum, the first twenty-two centimeters of the small intestine, it is further broken down into simpler substances.

The average stomach can hold about two and a half pints of food at a time. This is really a lot when you think of it. Of course we all try to put these limits to the test between late November and January first, when our stomachs are ready to go on permanent strike.

When you eat, it takes about ten minutes before your brain will register that you are satisfied. If you eat slowly, you will feel full before you feel overfull. If you go beyond your limits, you will likely become intimately familiar with the furnishings in the nearest bathroom. The most common cause for vomiting is eating or drinking too much.

Feeling full has a lot to do with how much you eat, but it also depends on the type of food you consume. When you eat a meal high in carbohydrates, the digestion begins in your mouth and is completed in your small intestine. The carbohydrates pass through the digestive system quickly and stay in your small intestine for less than an hour.

A high-fat meal is another story altogether. A fat-rich meal will make you feel fuller longer, because fats take longer to digest. Fats can remain in the gastrointestinal tract for hours. The digestion of fats doesn't even begin until the food reaches the small intestine. It may take ten hours for a fat-rich meal to be fully digested and absorbed.

If you eat a diet high in fat, which is arguably a definition of being an average American, you are most likely eating when there is still a significant amount of food going through the process of digestion. You may never experience true hunger because you are always full. You will be making your decisions about when and what to eat based on your mind and senses instead of your bodily signals.

An animal in its natural habitat will not eat until it is overfull. For example, when a horse is in the wild, its main function is to graze to maintain a consistent level of energy. However, when it is in captivity and sees a bucket of grain, it can literally eat itself to death. There is no work involved in getting the bucket of grain, and eaten all at once, it has too much energy value. Even though a horse's main function is to eat, nature never intended for it to live in stalls and have its food handed to it in a silver bucket.

Humans, on the other hand, whether in captivity or not, do not always know when to quit. Most Americans overeat, and obesity is one of the leading causes of heart disease.

FUNNY BONE

You've said it dozens of times in the past. "I don't mean funny ha! ha! ... I mean funny peculiar." Although you've probably been responding to a raised eyebrow following an innocent remark, few colloquial expressions describe the funny bone as aptly as this phrase. For sure, a funny-bone experience doesn't illicit joy, nor does it usually bring out a good cry. In spite of its name, it's interesting that, anatomically, the funny bone has little to do with comedy. Some may suspect the name "funny bone" was coined by doctors who noted its proximity to the humerus, a bone in the arm. But this is a stretch, especially when you consider the funny bone is not really a bone. Yet the moniker "funny bone" is not as much of a paradox as it might seem.

Remember when you were a child and you fell or had some other mishap that startled you more than it hurt? After each event your first response was to look at the reaction of your parents with a stunned blank stare. If your parents smiled, you laughed. If your parents looked horrified you cried. Similarly, your personal response to hitting your funny bone is directly related to not only how hard it's hit (a real wallop will send you into an orbit of pain no matter what your mental status), but how ready you were to laugh before it happened is also a factor in how you will react. If

you're happy, you'll probably laugh. If you're sad, you'll undoubtedly suffer some discomfort. Here's how it works.

The principal nerve that controls the muscles of your thumb, pinky finger, and one half of your ring finger is called the ulnar nerve. Normal anatomical variation allows for 10 percent of us to have our thumb and all of the little finger plus all of the ring finger and one half of the middle finger controlled by the ulnar nerve. When the ulnar is bumped, the feeling of "pins and needles" (called paresthesia) is felt in our fifth and fourth fingers (for some, the middle finger, too) and in the palm of our hand. Normally, the ulnar nerve travels from our spinal cord, through our shoulder and upper arm, and over our elbow to reach our hand. The funny bone is actually a place or a region in this nerve's path. Its precise location is on the back and medial side (armpit side) of our elbow. If you carefully feel this area with your finger you'll note a bony ridge that protrudes on the armpit side of your elbow. The ulnar nerve lies in an unprotected groove between this bump (medial epicondyle) and the point of our elbow (olecranon process), about one quarter inch beneath the surface of the skin. The nerve's vulnerability to outside trauma is based on a lack of overhead bony protection here. This position is coupled with the inevitability of the ulnar nerve becoming entrapped against an underlying bone (the humerus) when an outside force hits.

The fact is that everyone of us strikes his/her funny bone at one time or another, and most of us feel the immediate sensations from the blow. Some people liken the sensation to that of shaking hands with a prankster concealing a joy buzzer in his hand. Ultimately, our reaction to a minor blow to the funny bone is predicated, in part, on the mood we are in. If we are happy when we bump our funny bone, neurotransmitters in our brain dampen the discomfort and help us to focus on the lighter side of the pins and needles feeling. The numbness in our fingers is certainly real, but our threshold for discomfort becomes much higher. The reverse is true if we are depressed when we bang our elbow. Under this emotional circumstance our brain has a tendency to allow every negative aspect of the funny-bone experience to filter through. The result is a heightened sense of numbness and pain. If there is a moral attached to this experience, it is this. While one cannot usually plan accidents to elbows, if you bang yours, try to smile while doing so (think funny-haha!); chances are your positive emotion will take some of the discomfort away. Hence the true meaning of the term "funny bone."

But what about those of us who say we've hit our elbows and have never felt a funny-bone sensation? The answer is wait and see. Some 2–5 percent of us have a delayed reaction to a funny-bone traumatic episode. This delayed response is called tardy palsy. In this situation sensations of pins and needles often develop years after the causative event.

GOOSEBUMPS

Goosebumps, also called gooseflesh, got their name because of their resemblance to the skin of a plucked goose. A goosebump is an erection of a hair follicle that comes in response to a local cold or tactile stimulus or a frightening or thrilling emotion.

Even though parents everywhere will disagree with me, when you are frightened—when, for example, your two-year-old decides to climb the stairs from the outside railing for the third time—the hair on your head does not really stand up on end like you see it do on characters in the movies. The hair on your arms and legs, however, will stand up because the tiny arrector pili muscles (a Latin word for "erector of hair") pull on the hair follicles.

If we were as hairy now as we were in caveman days, we would probably look much like a dog or cat with its hackles raised. So scientists interested in evolutionary theories about the body have surmised that the goosebump effect could be another form of the fight or flight response. Back in our early days as a species we might very well have used the raising of the hair to look bigger and scarier, like dogs and cats do today.

Being extremely cold will also cause goosebumps. This may also stem from our early evolutionary days. The raised hair follicles may have helped us keep warm, since the fluffed-out hair would trap warmth close to the body. It could also be that the cold air stimulates cold receptors in the skin, which sends messages to the brain that in turn will signal blood vessels and the arrector pili muscles to constrict to hold in the warmth. Either way, it is a mechanism of adapting to our environment without benefit of down comforters, woolen sweaters, or electric blankets.

Alcohol will curtail the onset or range of a goosebump reaction. Smokers and coffee drinkers also tend not to be as quick to goosebump.

If you have low blood sugar, you will be much more apt to get goosebumps, because the body's resting heat production is reduced, which will activate heat conservation mechanisms such as gooseflesh.

HANGOVER

The main character in the popular film *Arthur* uses his role to characterize a hangover so successfully that his portrayal is truly vintage realism. As viewers, we can empathize with him and his throbbing headache, nausea, stomach upset, cotton mouth, thirst, diarrhea, cramping, fatigue, and irritability. In ninety minutes, Hollywood captures the essence of what hundreds of thousands of us feel after a weekend binge that's usually followed by a sworn commitment to never drink alcohol again. But despite good intentions we should avoid making promises that create self-imposed stress. Arthur's role conveys the little-known fact that drinking while experiencing guilt and anxiety is more apt to lead to a serious hangover than drinking when we're footloose and fancy free. The reason for this difference is that even while we are sober, stress causes constant nerve stimulation in our midbrain and hinders our ability to relax. This bombardment generates hangoverlike symptoms of malaise and nausea in us even before we take a drop of alcohol!

Once alcohol enters our bloodstream, more than 90 percent of it must be detoxified by our liver. There is no way to speed up this process. Efforts to sober up like drinking black coffee and taking cold showers may help us empty our bladder, but do nothing to reduce our intoxication or minimize the hangover to come. The average party drinker who usually consumes one ounce of alcohol every twenty to thirty minutes—a rate that is four times faster than what the liver can handle—should take note of this. The liver is so overworked by this that there is a delayed clearing of the broken-down alcohol by-products (metabolites) from our blood even after all the intact alcohol is gone! Simply put, a hangover is really a syndrome of symptoms arising from the presence of alcohol breakdown products in our body. Furthermore, the extent to which the hangover symptoms persist—usually up to ten hours—has a direct correlation with the time it takes for us to totally eliminate metabolites from our blood. A long-held belief is that the hair of the dog, drinking more alcohol, can help cure a hangover. The truth is, treating a hangover with alcohol simply adds more metabolites, postpones recovery, and makes it worse. The metabolite story, however, is only half of the cause of a hangover. Alcohol contaminants commercially placed inside our drink make up the rest of the story.

Alcohol is produced from the fermentation of carbohydrates in the presence of yeast. Yet the alcohol we usually buy (ethanol) is purposefully not chemically pure. For retail sale, ethanol contains many substances that contribute to the specific color and flavor of the type of spirit that we enjoy. The alcohol industry calls these elements congeners. Arguably, evidence exists that congeners are as important as alcohol waste products in triggering hangovers. The greatest likelihood of getting a hangover is from drinking liquor that's the darkest (that has greatest number of congeners). Bourbon, brandy, and scotch head this list. White wine, gin, and vodka (the least offensive) have a minimum of congeners in their formulation. Red wines deliver a double whammy to the drinker, because not only are they rich in congeners, but they contain high amounts of the headache-producing amino acid tyramine. Tyramine is a histamine-like substance that can cause crippling headaches.

OK, you know what brings on the hangover. What causes its symptoms? Our throbbing headache is not only related to alcohol's dilation effect on the blood vessels in our brain, but also to the dramatic effect it has on lowering our blood sugar. Alcohol causes an overproduction of insulin in our body. This sudden availability of insulin, called the hypoglycemic effect, drives our blood sugar into our body's storage cells, leaving us inappropriately sugar deprived and headache prone. To create the worst possible humdinger hangover, drink on an empty stomach and be sure to sip a sweet wine or liqueur. The sugared alcohol will totally fool the body into thinking it needs even less sugar than is appropriate for our already existing low blood sugar taste. The ultimate effect of this combination is that we inadvertently create a super-intensive molotov-cocktail headache!

The thirsty, dehydrated sensation that accompanies nearly every hangover is caused by the strong diuretic effect that alcohol has on our kidneys. Normally, the body preserves water through the action of a hormone called ADH (antidiuretic hormone). ADH is blocked by alcohol, causing our body to release water through our bladder. A commonly held misconception is that we lose the same amount of body water that we drink. If this eye-for-an-eye theory were true, then when we drink a six-pack, we should loose six times twelve ounces, or approximately two liters of fluid. The reality is, we lose nearly three times what we drink! A six pack could cost us 6 liters of fluid and leave us droolless, with a cotton mouth.

The stomach upset, nausea, cramping, and diarrhea that accompany every first-rate hangover are caused by the increased secretion of hydrochloric acid in our stomach. It's truly amazing how resistant our tummy is to alcohol despite these symptoms. The same amount of acid that our stomach usually secretes during an alcohol bash, if spilled on our shoe, would eat a hole through the leather to our sole in a matter of minutes. It's understandable, then, that frequent alcohol hangovers could do the same to our stomach (and our soul) if we're not careful.

When it comes to hangover cures and remedies, before we start toasting the numerous recommendations that history has recorded, we should know that the FDA has found no present or past over-the-counter product that relieves the symptoms of a hangover. This finding includes the popular belief that fruit juices, which contain a form of sugar called fructose, or honey, which is a concentrated source of fructose, help.

Then if after-hangover care doesn't work, what about taking an aspirin the night before a binge to help prevent a headache? There is some evidence that the salicylates in aspirin help, but only with the headache symptom. However, this partial free ticket may be outweighed by aspirin's propensity to cause stomach irritation. The best prevention of a hangover may be mixing ourselves a Virgin Mary or a Shirley Temple for a second or third round. Otherwise, hangovers have a habit of counting drinks even when we don't.

HEADACHES

There are almost as many theories about headaches as there are headache sufferers. When you consider that approximately 45 million Americans experience headaches each year, you shouldn't be surprised to find the explanations a bit baffling.

No one has to describe a headache to you if you have ever experienced one. But just so we are on the same wavelength: There is a vise-on-the-head headache, the pounding-hammer headache, the "my face is going to explode any minute" headache, the left side headache, the right side headache, the bug-eyed headache, the "I want to kill somebody headache," and the "don't breathe—you are being too loud" headache.

Headaches are a documented plague that have been around for at least two thousand years. In medieval times doctors would open a patient's skull with a chisel and hammer to cure a headache. Who knows, maybe they thought they could distract the patient, who might have preferred this torture to the throbbing migraine.

Another remedy was to rub the patient's head with a certain species of toad. It reminds me of the giraffe repellent an uncle teased me about when I was a child. When I asked him how it worked, he pointed to my front lawn and said, "See, there are no giraffes."

There are at least three kinds of headaches scientists have

categorized in addition to the type of headaches associated with sinusitus, the common cold, and flu. They are tension headaches, migraines, and cluster headaches. There are some scientists and practitioners who feel tension is partially to blame in all three types of headaches, but there are distinctions in how the brain reacts that would support the theory that different things are going on with each type of ailment.

If you get a headache every time your mother-in-law gives you that tight-lipped glare that you know means she wishes you were everything you are not, you are probably suffering from tension. Tension headaches do not always happen the minute you feel stressed. It is usually during the letdown period after the stress that you develop all the symptoms. So if your mother-in-law's glare gives you a delayed reaction, you might want to consider some of the many techniques used to reduce stress before it can get the better of you.

Check your posture. Bad posture may make you more prone to tension headaches caused by muscle contraction. If you engage in any prolonged sitting activity like typing, you need to stretch your muscles so that they do not tense up and cause a headache. Many people have found that relaxation techniques are very helpful in reducing stress-related headaches. If you enjoy the sounds of a tape of nature or soft music with guided imagery, you might be able to talk yourself out of your pain.

Acupressure is another alternative approach to pain medication that some people swear reduces muscular tension and eliminates headaches. With acupressure you use your fingers to put pressure on certain key points related to meridians in your body that are supposed to release energy. The pressure points related to headaches are found between the thumb and index finger and at the base of the skull.

Aerobic exercise is a boon for tension headache sufferers because it increases beta endomorphins, a natural pain reliever in the body. Some people may find their headache pain increases with exercise, which means they may have something other than a tension or muscle contraction problem.

Migraine or vascular headaches are the second most common form of headache and afflict over 15 percent of American adults. The first symptoms can develop any time between the ages of five and thirty but usually develop during puberty.

Migraine headaches involve constricted blood vessels inside the skull which for several reasons suddenly expand. The expansion irritates nerves surrounding the vessels and can cause excruciating pain and other symptoms like severe throbbing, pain on one side of the head, nausea, vomiting, cold hands, dizziness, and sensitivity to light and noise. If you think that sounds strangely similar to a hangover, you are not wrong. Actually many migrainers inadvertently bring on their symptoms by the foods they eat and other migraine triggers.

There is a strong correlation between certain food sensitivities and migraine headaches. Foods that contain the chemical tyramine, which would include chocolate, peanuts, aged cheese, alcohol, food preservatives, monosodium glutamate (MSG), and nitrates, can trigger migraines, because they cause vasodilation (blood vessel expansion). They also cause spasms of the blood vessels in the brain of people with a likelihood of getting headaches. Other foods that are high in tyramine are ripe avocados, ripe bananas, figs, dried fish, and pickled herring.

People with classic types of migraines have problems with their vision before they actually have the pain of the headache. They may also feel confused and light-headed and have difficulty concentrating. In some people, these classic migraine symptoms can be triggered by a linear pattern in wallpaper, window blinds, or any kind of grid with a monotonous design.

Scientists are now trying to find the link between an imbalance of certain biochemicals or neurotransmitters in the brain and headaches, especially migraines. As with many of our problematic symptoms, the neurotransmitter serotonin seems to play a role. In addition to its other jobs as a chemical messenger between neurons, serotonin regulates the constriction and dilation of blood vessels.

There are drugs that will help relieve migraine headaches. But with any kind of pharmacological approach there is always the danger of the drug eventually causing the problem it was meant to cure. There is an actual case of a woman who was on pain relievers for forty years. When she inadvertently went cold turkey, her symptoms disappeared almost immediately.

Some people find relief from headaches by cutting out salt from their diet. If a person is susceptible, even a small amount of salt can trigger a migraine. Salt causes a hormone response that can lead to dilation and expansion of the blood vessels. If you cut down on salt, you can also reduce susceptibility to other migraine triggers.

Perhaps one of the best natural approaches to the relief of migraine headaches is biofeedback. When it first was introduced it was probably put in the category of computerized voodoo, but it is now a close second choice to drug therapy. The process of bio-feedback—which has been compared to being hooked up to a lie detector machine—enables you to learn to control the autonomic nervous system, which is what governs "involuntary" body processes like blood vessel dilation. Biofeedback is also designed to teach you to relax deeply. This will eliminate the tension component of many migraine headaches.

Cluster headaches are the least common type. It is a good thing, too, because they can be so excruciating that people have been moved to acts of violence by them. They appear in cycles at a particular time of the day or in groups at a particular time of the year, and are believed to be regulated by the hypothalamus. The hypothalamus is another part of the brain sensitive to serotonin.

Perhaps the most baffling type of headache is the "not to-night, dear," kind. This is not just a fabrication of wives or husbands who suddenly find after twenty years that their spouses do not even closely resemble their physical ideal. There are actually headaches triggered by the act of sex. This syndrome has a name: cephalagia. It comes on with the force of a severe migraine during sex, just at or before the point of orgasm.

There are many possible reasons why this headache occurs. It may be brought on by muscle contraction in the neck and upper body during intercourse. It may also be caused by the contraction of blood vessels in the head and neck. Of course, trying to beat the world's record for contorted lovemaking positions can trigger a headache as well.

Headaches may be a modern phenomenon. They do not serve any apparent purpose that would enhance our quality of life. It seems they are a sign, as Andrew Elmore, a behaviorial medicine specialist affiliated with the Mt. Sinai Headache Clinic, laments, that the human nervous system is too primitive to deal with the modern world. Maybe when we were designed, the Grand Engineer could not possibly have foreseen the kind of world we have created for ourselves.

HEARTBURN

hat's heartburn? Does our heart really burn? Does it cause something else to ignite? When we're being romantic, we often describe our cardiac bonfires to our loved one, but when we're not, we complain and run for the Tums. Regardless of our reaction to heartburn, doctors know sparks and flames are elements of emotion, not physiology. *Heartburn* is an actual backing-up of the acids from our stomach. This unpleasant chemical retreat usually enters and leaves its burning residue in our food pipe, or esophagus. If the acids travel all the way up to our mouth, causing a hot, bitter, or sour liquid taste (sorry, I know it's a repulsive thought), we call it *waterbrash*. For those lucky enough to have never experienced it, heartburn is a burning sensation beneath the breast bone. It normally affects more than one third of us at least once a month. Although it may radiate to our throat, neck, jaw, and even face, this burning symptom we feel usually begins near our heart. It's this anatomical positioning that has given rise to the term heartburn. Heartburn hits first at the base of the esophagus near the opening valve of the stomach, which lies behind our breast bone and not behind our navel, where most of us erroneously think our stomach sits!

Why do we get heartburn? The common reason is because we overextend our stomach with food. The resulting back pressure opens a muscular valve, called the cardiac sphincter, that's located between the bottom of our esophagus and the top of our stomach. When the sphincter opens, stomach acid moves into our esophagus and irritates its unprotected lining. Because of this absence of a protective coating, our symptoms begin within seconds of the esophagus' exposure to gastric acid. Incidentally, if the pressure from our overextended stomach is slightly less then the pressure necessary to open our cardiac sphincter, bending over or lying down will add just enough gravitational pull to open it and bring on the symptoms.

It's understandable that overeating may cause heartburn by making our cardiac sphincter bulge out, but what about the heartburn we get from taking just a few sips of a beverage or bites of a certain food? What does smoking, alcohol, coffee, onions, chocolate, or a greasy meal have in common that gives us symptoms even under normal stomach pressure conditions? The answer is, they all have ingredients that act similarly to the way a tickling feather on our nose causes us to sneeze. Caffeine, nicotine, and fat irritate our cardiac sphincter and cause it to open and our stomach muscles to contract. Heartburn usually arises from the increase in acid that's produced by the presence of these foodstuffs. This increased concentration of acid, pushed along by our contracting stomach muscles, finds its way through the open sphincter door and makes us feel like we have something similar to a smoldering campfire nestled behind our breast bone.

Although heartburn is usually associated with eating or overeating, there is a rather common anatomical condition that also brings on symptoms. It's called a sliding hiatal hernia. A hiatal hernia does not occur in our pelvic region, nor does it have anything to do with our reproductive system. We commonly confuse the terminology of an inguinal hernia (in our groin) with a hiatal hernia (in our abdomen), and they are quite different! Our stomach sits beneath our breathing muscle, the diaphragm. The diaphragm contains an opening called a hiatus, that the esophagus slips through on its way to our mouth. Occasionally, the stomach will try to move or slide through this opening meant for the esophagus. When this happens, we feel a momentary belt-tightening sensation around the portion of the stomach that is sliding through the diaphragm. The pressure generated above the squeezed section of the stomach pushes gastric acid back into our esophagus. This is a potential heartburn situation. A sliding hiatus hernia is found in about 40 percent of the population. Fortunately, however, most cases are asymptomatic and require no other treatment than a well-placed antacid. While we're talking about antacids, here's a quick tip. Antacids containing aluminum tend to cause constipation, while those with magnesium tend to cause diarrhea. It's ironic, then, that while we're trying to put out a fire in our upper gastrointestinal tract, we can upset our lower GI tract.

Next to diet and sliding hiatal hernias, pregnancy is the most common cause of heartburn. The hormonal changes that accompany pregnancy also diminish our stomach's motility and cause reverse contractile muscle waves to occur. The resulting regurgitation opens our cardiac sphincter and brings on heartburn. Although eating several small meals daily instead of three large ones is often recommended for relief, perhaps the most curious suggestion for the expecting mom is not what to take but what to do! I'll never forget the first time I visited birthing classes and saw a group of women in their second trimester flapping their arms and trying to fly! That's right, they had just returned from having lunch and were complaining of heartburn. The obstetric nurse had the entire group sit in a tailorlike fashion with their arms raised and then instructed them to lower their arms quickly and then bring their hands together over their head. This exercise was repeated several times. Much to my amazement, without the thrill and excitement of an actual airplane ride the flying exercise worked. Later I learned that the body mechanics of flapping help regulate both the pressure of the stomach and its contraction. One might feel a little ridiculous doing this regimen in front of others, but when it comes to putting out a pyrosis (heartburn), the flying exercise often takes off when most antacids leave us grounded!

HICCUPS

iccups, also called hiccoughs, are as common to our lives as yawning. They involve an involuntary contraction of the diaphragm, the muscle separating the abdomen and chest. When the diaphragm contracts, the vocal chords close quickly, which is what makes the funny "hiccuping" sound. Perhaps what is most interesting about hiccups is that, although we know what they are, no one really knows why they happen.

Hiccups seem to be induced by many different circumstances. If you eat or drink too fast, you might get a case of hiccups. If you are fatigued, nervous, pregnant, or an alcoholic, you can expect some hiccups somewhere along the way. If you happen to have an ant walking around on your eardrum, like one poor woman in Jerusalem, you can expect a pretty severe case of hiccups. At five times per minute, hers were maddening until doctors discovered the intruder. Evidently the little bug irritated the vagus nerve, which runs from the brain, through the ear, and down into the abdomen. The hiccups were probably a form of physiological counterattack.

Most of the time hiccups do not indicate anything as important as an invasion from the insect kingdom. They usually stop in a few minutes whether you do anything about them or not.

There was, however, one case of hiccups listed in the Guinness Book of World Records that lasted for sixty years. Charles Osborne of Anthon, Iowa started hiccuping in 1922 after slaughtering a hog, and he must have hiccupped at least 430 million times. He said he was able to live a fairly normal life during which he had two wives and eight children. He did have some difficulty keeping his false teeth in his mouth.

His case seems a bit suspicious. The explanation might be that he was under some kind of hog curse. Hogs are supposed to be highly intelligent, and so far no one has come up with anything better.

For those people who can't accept that most hiccups go away on their own, there are many remedies. Although they are considered to be old wives' tales, many people swear by them. If you drink a liquid from the opposite side of the glass you should be able to stop your hiccups. You can take a spoonful of sugar or blow into a paperbag. The most popular remedy is being scared by someone so you can shock your hiccups away, but you could also stand on your head. No matter what you do, within five minutes you should be miraculously cured.

HUNGER

For many of us eating is more of a hobby than an important bodily function. We eat to satisfy our taste buds, our emotional needs, and our need for entertainment. It is not surprising that many of us wouldn't know a true hunger pang if it bit us. It is difficult to separate hunger from appetite which is the (spl)urge to eat specific foods.

Do you become hungry when you pass a bakery and are knocked off your feet by the smell of freshly baked cookies? Most likely, unless you haven't eaten for several hours, you are responding to sensory stimulation and your memory of how much pleasure is in store for you if you indulge. Bakers know this, so they usually strategically place their ovens where they will generate the most odors.

Actual hunger is caused when our blood sugar is low and our stomachs are empty. The brain receives a signal in the hypothalamus, a part of the lower brain that regulates hunger, thirst, sleep, and sexual behavior, which causes the muscles in the stomach wall to contract. This is the hunger "pang," which for dieters is either a signal that the diet is working or that it is nearing its end.

When human beings are deprived of food, the hypothalamus—the internal regulator of the central nervous system—has to find a way to create internal balance. The physiological responses include a decrease in blood pressure, an increase in armpit tem-

perature, an increase in saliva, an increase in the number and rate of stomach contractions, and a decrease in respiration rate. Just ask any fast-food cashier during the lunch rush, and you will hear that this is not always a pretty sight.

When people are hungry their hypothalamus will trigger the feeding response, which becomes a primary urge that must be satisfied. Hungry people are often irritable and can even become irrational as the drop in blood sugar triggers biochemical responses in the brain.

For some people feelings of hunger are actually caused by the desire to chew. Chewing releases tension, whether it is chewing pencils, pens, chair legs, or large quantities of crunchy foods. Researchers are trying to discover nonfattening chewing alternatives like fibrous low-calorie chew sticks. Perhaps they will even come out with a line of chew toys for adults or rawhide bones in the shape of celery sticks.

For some people even thinking about food can be fattening. Studies of obese people have shown that when certain people think about food or see certain foods, their level of insulin—the hormone which regulates blood sugar—increases. This stimulates the hunger center, causing the person to crave more food even though their stomach might be adequately filled.

This can have devastating effects on people who watch a great deal of television. Commercials can be very fattening, especially on Saturday morning. Avoiding certain food cues can prevent the biochemical changes that put some people at a gastronomic disadvantage, but in our world this is not always a simple task. We are not unlike Pavlov's dogs, who learned to salivate at the sound of a bell. Hypersensitive eaters who have a conditioned insulin response need to learn new behavior to control the insulin surges. Taking a walk or having a drink of water helps.

INSOMNIA

I t is 1:30 A.M. You have been in bed since eleven trying to drift into a peaceful slumber. You have thought pleasant thoughts, and have counted sheep until they were too tired to go on. No matter what you do, as soon as you think you have it licked, your eyes pop open and you stare at the stucco on your ceiling.

For the next hour you try to avoid the clock. Every time you see it, you realize you are not sleeping. You cover your head with your new feather pillow, which was touted as a sure remedy for sleeplessness. As far as you know you fall asleep but you find yourself staring at the ceiling again at least two hours before you need to get up. You throw the clock across the room, get out of bed, and start your day feeling cranky and irritable.

The large majority of people who suffer from insomnia, or chronic sleeplessness, are over the age of fifty. Part of the problem is that as we age our metabolism slows down and we need less sleep. Despite this fact we have been conditioned to expect a certain amount of sleep and will rely on the clock rather than our bodies to tell us what we need.

If we think we are not getting enough sleep, we may become a bit obsessed about it. We will worry when we do not drift off like we used to, or when we wake up earlier, which only makes things worse.

Another problem for older people is that there are interruptions to sleep that are a natural result of the aging process. Many people have pain in joints or muscles that can keep them from reaching deep levels of sleep.

Some people also have leg twitches called nocturnal myoclonus that can cause restlessness. These spasms are not enough to wake a person up fully, but they are distracting. These twitches seem to increase with age. If you can determine that this is interrupting your sleep, your doctor may be able to prescribe medication to reduce the problem.

Sleep apnea is another problem for sleepers that may go unnoticed. This is when there is a pause in breathing during the night, usually caused by fatty tissue that has accumulated in the larynx and palate. The remedy for this is typically to lose weight.

One problem for older insomniacs is that their expectation of what constitutes a good night's sleep can lead them to do things that actually work against them. Trying to make up for what they think is lost sleep by taking naps during the day might make them unable to sleep at night. Some people benefit from short naps during the day, which are part of the overall picture of their sleep pattern. But not everyone needs them.

Insomnia is by no means confined to the over-fifty set. Even a high school student can have a sleepless night over an impending final exam. One study has shown that more than 70 percent of people of all age ranges who have trouble sleeping have some type of emotional disturbance or anxiety. Anxiety, which comes from a Greek root word meaning "to strangle," is a very common generalized feeling of foreboding and nervousness that can come about from life circumstances and stress or a biochemical imbalance. One of the main symptoms of anxiety is sleep disturbance.

For example, have you ever found yourself awakened by something at four A.M. only to find you can't get back to sleep? You

begin to think about bills unpaid, letters unwritten, and all the things you should have done with your life. When you wake up again the world tends to look a lot better than it did during your middle-of-the-night panic attack.

Your insomnia is a symptom of your very real anxiety. During your waking state you might be harboring unexpressed feelings that need to get worked out. If you find a way to get to the heart of the matter, you will usually find that your sleep will return to normal.

A few bouts with insomnia might make you cranky, but prolonged sleep deprivation can be downright harmful. Studies have shown that after only twenty-four hours of lost sleep a person will function much less efficiently than normal. After ten sleepless days he will have trouble functioning or carrying out any mental or physical tasks. Cults and unscrupulous police interrogators have been known to intentionally cause sleeplessness in a person to make brainwashing or the extraction of a confession easier. After a period of time a sleep-deprived person will become impressionable and will completely lack willpower. Constant interruptions of deep REM (Rapid Eye Movement) sleep can have the same impact. A person reaches the REM dream state about one hour after falling to sleep and has about five or more intervals of REM during the sleep period. Although we know very little about dreams and REM sleep, we do know they are somehow connected to how we learn information. Studies have shown that people deprived of REM sleep are less able to make decisions, assimilate new information and are at increased heart disease risk.

To avoid insomnia and to get a good night's sleep you should: hire a babysitter and go to a hotel if you have a young family, or forget about it for a couple of years; learn to meditate, if it will draw your attention away from your worries; eat something light like a protein snack before going to bed, so your working digestive system will make you sleepy; get some exercise some time during the day but not too close to bedtime; make sure you have a comfortable mattress; and make sure you have a compatible spouse or significant other.

Don't leave the television on; your mind sometimes picks up images and sounds and incorporates them into your dreams. Don't drink alcohol before going to bed. It may relax you enough to fall asleep, but it will have a rebound effect. In a few hours your eyes will pop wide open and you will begin your cycle of insomnia all over again. Finally, work through all your anxieties, fears, and hidden motivations. Maybe a good psychoanalyst could help you understand the connection between the subconscious and insomnia, but for now it is best not to lose any sleep over it.

ITCHES

There really aren't too many situations in life that get under our skin and drive us loony quite like an itch. An itch has a habit of coming at the wrong time and appearing in places that are nearly always difficult and awkward to reach. In medicine, we usually refer to itching, or pruritus, as a benign condition. However, the true definition of "benign" is "something of a kind disposition," and I don't think anyone would define an itch that way.

What is an itch and what causes it? The classic explanation is that an itch is a sensation that instinctively makes us scratch. While the mental torture a good itch causes may need little description, the usual causes of itching are nearly as varied as the intensity of the itch itself. Although almost any physical or chemical stimulus to the skin can cause itching, there are really two basic types of body responses that lead to most of our itching episodes. One is sensory and the other is allergic.

The sensory itch is the root of such irritating questions as "Why does my head itch when I have a hat on?" "Why does my leg itch under my cast?" and "Why does my skin itch when my facial beard or bikini hair line grows back?" Here's how the sensory itch works. It is initiated by one type of nerve receptor, the Merkel's disc. Merkel's discs are pressure plate receptors that sit in our outer epidermal skin layer. They respond slowly to minor external pressure such as the burden we receive from a hat or a cast. Nerve signals generated by the pressure from these objects are transmitted to our brain. If the pressure is familiar to our brain, as with a loving touch or the constant pressure of a shoe or sock, then we subconsciously tolerate it. If the pressure is not familiar to us, as with the occasional use of a hat or the existence of a cast, then our brain interprets the pressure signals as muddled crosstalk. Once the itch begins, it's reproduction is passed from the Merkel's disc to our pain receptors, which continue the process. Our brain then interprets this vague input as a nuisance touch on our skin and sends a message to scratch it away. If we constantly wore a hat or a cast, this pressure would be familiar to our brain and the itch would not likely occur.

It's interesting that a woolen hat, like a ski cap, is exceptionally prone to cause itching. The reason is because the band of the cap not only activates the Merkel's discs, but the woolen fibers also directly tickle the nerve endings wrapped around our hair shafts. This double stimulation causes our woolen cap to give us intense itching fits.

Incidentally, this tickling of our hair shafts by woolen cap fibers is the same mechanism that initiates intense itching when our hair starts to regrow along our bikini line or after we have shaved a beard. As you've probably surmised, a sensory itch has a lot to do with adaptation. Our body doesn't like sudden changes like new pressure points from a hat, hair regrowth after a respite, or even a wisp of air against our skin. When these things happen, our brain responds with an exploratory scratch that tries to remove the offending agent.

Why does cold seem to help the sensory itch? We can use the ski cap to demonstrate what happens. When we're exposed to real cold weather our nerve receptors are numbed and carry messages very slowly. As soon as we work up a sweat and generate warmth in our scalp or get toasty inside the lodge, our nerves start firing and itching begins. Individually, though, heat and dryness also tend to lower our threshold for itching. Heat works by dilating our blood vessels, therefore supplying our nerves with more blood to enhance their transmission. Dryness irritates us by creating a parched environment on our skin that aids in pressure reception.

But what about the itch-scratch-itch cycle: Why do I keep scratching once I start? Our skin not only contains fibers for touch and pressure, but also contains free nerve-ending receptors that are primarily responsible for pain. The point here is that an itch and a pain sensation are both carried by the same nerve fiber. After the initial itch, which begins with the Merkel's disc, our pain fibers get stimulated by our scratching. The resulting message informs our brain that an annoyance is either removed or still there. If the stimulus is still present, or, paradoxically, if we've created one by our scratching, then we'll respond with another scratch. The itch-scratch-itch cycle continues until we find a way to control our fingers and stop the stimulation. You can easily set off this phenomenon by scratching the back of your hand. Within seconds you'll have an urge to scratch again. You can thank your pain fibers for this feeling!

How does an allergic itch differ from a sensory itch, you ask? First, the stimulus is different. An allergic itch is not pressure sensitive and can be brought on by certain types of medication. Codeine, sulphur, and antibiotics are a few common ones that will set off an allergic itch. Other common causes are insect bites or foreign bodies that irritate our immune system. The key to the allergic itch is that it's brought on by something that triggers our body's principle allergic response chemical, histamine. Histamine is stored in our immune system cells and is released when our brain senses an exposure to a foreign body. Histamine, as a vanguard of our body's defense system, immediately causes localized blood vessel dilation (redness), passage of fluid through our cell walls (wheal formation), and stimulation of local free nerve-ending pain fibers (flaring and itching). This source of body itch continues until the histamine is either removed by the body naturally (a bee or mosquito bite takes eighteen to twenty-four hours) or by the use of antihistamine medication, which usually works within hours. Unlike the sensory itch where the pain receptor helps propagate the itch-scratch-itch cycle, in the allergic itch, this cycle is continued by our spreading histamine below the surface of our skin through our scratching.

Aside from the causes of itching already explained, perhaps the single most common and misunderstood itch is the one caused by our scalp when we haven't shampooed our hair for several days. As our hair starts to itch, many of us immediately suspect that we have a scalp disease like seborrheic dermatitis, which is an overactivity of the scalp's sebaceous, or oil-producing glands, or some sort of contagious dandruff. Our usual anxious response is to pick up a tar-based shampoo on our next visit to the drug store. The good news is that most of the time our sebaceous glands are working fine. It's just that their oily residue, along with the normal daily buildup of soap, hair spray, air pollutants, and dead skin, need to be prevented from stimulating our hair follicle nerve fibers. Under most circumstances a shower works as well as a coal tar shampoo.

A final note: Why does our nose itch so often for no apparent reason? There are many possibilities, but the most common one involves moisture and bacteria. Fortunately, our personal hygiene has little to do with this little nuisance. The bacteria I speak of is the normal flora that we have on our skin. When our nose becomes dry due to decreased external humidity, especially in the winter, our body naturally tries to compensate by warming incoming air with moist heat from our nose. This moist nasal air makes for a great condo environment in which our body's bacteria stay warm. It also creates a great environment for our bacteria to tickle us enough to cause an itch. If these bacterial freeloaders trouble you, get a humidifier for your house. Nasal sprays may seem like an instant itch remedy, but like back scratchers, they ultimately make matters worse by stimulating and not relieving.

LAUGHTER

Laughter is important for your health. Although stoic types might consider laughing to be frivolous, it is a proven fact that a good hearty laugh can improve performance and relieve pain.

Of course there are different types of laughs. There are reflex laughs, like when someone tickles you under your armpit or on the bottom of your feet.

And there are laughs triggered by whatever it is that you find amusing. While laughter is common to all human beings, a sense of humor is a different story.

Scientists such as Charles Darwin have been fascinated with laughter's physiological and societal implications. Darwin believed laughter, which occurs in infants as young as five weeks, was an evolutionary means to reward parental caretaking, insuring survival of the species. The mechanism of laughter is so opposite to screaming and cries of distress, even in patterns of respiration, that he felt it could only be interpreted as a sign of well-being.

Darwin also viewed laughter as a means of discharging surplus tension or mental excitation that will accumulate if not properly vented. Freud also believed laughter is closely associated with lust. Pent up tension due to inhibition is released in the morally innocent form of a joke. Laughter can actually restore balance and equilibrium and stimulate circulation and produce a sense of well-being.

When you laugh, electrical impulses are triggered by nerves in your brain. This sets off chemical reactions. Your endocrine (glandular) system orders your brain to secrete natural tranquilizers and painkillers, such as endorphins and enkephalines.

Styles of laughter differ from coy little giggles to guffaws. Some people actually sound like they are choking, and others sound like braying donkeys. Laughs are as individual as people. The sounds of laughter are produced by deep inhalation of air followed by short, spasmodic contractions of the diaphragm. The mechanism is the same for all, but most likely heredity and your mental state will determine what type of laugh category you will fall within.

Sometimes something is so side-splittingly funny that you find yourself laughing and crying at the same time. This is because when you laugh, your entire body convulses. When this happens, the tear-producing lacrimal glands are stimulated to force out small drops of moisture.

No one has a surefire formula for what is funny. Stand-up comedians steal from each other to try to capture the laughs but find that sometimes it isn't the joke that is funny, it's the delivery. One theory is that, at least in infants, incongruence provokes laughter. When a baby sees something that does not fit in with their sense of reality, once they determine they are not in any danger, they will laugh out of relief.

Laughter can be contagious. Think back to a time when you were in a church, synagogue, or school, where it would be totally inappropriate to laugh out loud, and you will probably remember a horrendous case of the giggles.

Dr. Norman Cousins, in his book *Anatomy of an Illness as Perceived by the Patient,* claims laughter helped him regain his health. His evidence was so overwhelming that many hospitals now have laughing libraries so patients, particularly those with cancer, can use laughter as part of their therapy.

LOSS OF BALANCE

Those of us who are reasonably healthy don't have to consciously worry about how to remain upright without falling. Unless, of course, we are pulled over after a few too many drinks and asked to walk a straight line. Then we can appreciate how the brain, when it is functioning unimpaired, so effortlessly uses the senses of touch and vision and an intricate system of fluid-filled canals in the inner ear to keep us walking the straight and narrow.

Our skin, which is the main organ of touch, forms a boundary between our inner world and our outer environment. It accounts for 20 percent of our body weight and is made up of tiny sensory organs. It gives us an awareness of how we relate to other physical things.

There is a component of touch called kinesthesis that senses and responds to movement. Each muscle, tendon, and joint in our bodies has what are called proprioceptive receptors, which tell the brain what is happening to us every time we move. The body will automatically help us change our movement to adapt to this information. If we had to make every decision of this kind consciously, we would spend most of our time on our backsides.

Vision is important to our sense of balance for the information it provides about the body's position in relationship to its surroundings. It is important but not vital. Sightless people can develop their sense of touch to compensate for their loss of vision and still maintain their balance.

The vestibular system in the inner ear is the most important ingredient for proper balance. It is made up of five tiny fluid-filled canals in each ear that work like a carpenter's level. Three of the canals, which make up what is called the labyrinth, help maintain equilibrium in the body as it moves back and forth, up and down, and side to side. When the head moves, the fluid shifts and bends tiny hairlike receptors in each of the canals, sending messages to the brain. The brain then sends messages telling the body how to compensate and shift position.

The vestibular system is vital to our ability to "see straight." As your head and eyes shift to take in visual information, the vestibular system works with the nerve endings at the base of the neck to send messages to the brain to compensate for the movement. For example, if you move your head back and forth quickly while reading a page of a book, you can still make out the words. If you move the book back and forth, the words will be a blur, as they are not maintained within your field of vision.

As a society we typically overload our senses of vision and hearing through lack of physical activity and an overreliance on television, books, and other forms of media. This could theoretically cause our sense of balance to atrophy. Scientists have discovered that our senses work together to respond to movement. When we use our whole bodies and all of our senses, we can learn much more quickly than if we passively watch a how-to video. So the more sedentary we become, the less finely tuned we will be.

Even if you are the quintessential couch potato, you can always improve your sense of balance through a simple exercise. If you find your center of gravity you can consciously align your body with that focal point. Your center point can be found by placing the palm of your left hand on your abdomen right below the navel and placing the back of the other hand on the small of the back. The point at the center of the two hands is the point from which balance and movement stem.

Some people believe that finding your center point is the first step toward achieving the elusive balance of mind, body, and spirit. Yoga practitioners consider alignment and physical balance to be a key to health, vitality, and long life.

If you have ever been pregnant, you know how it feels to have a major shift in your center of gravity. For pregnant women, balance is directly proportional to how well they can see their toes. When the body is out of alignment, it is more likely that the information-gathering mechanisms will misread the input they are receiving, making it very easy to fall.

Falling is often very hazardous to your health. There are more than thirteen thousand fatalities in the United States each year from falls, whether on purpose or otherwise. When human beings fall from any great height, as sophisticated as our internal mechanism for maintaining balance might be, we usually tumble uncontrollably. We are as likely to fall on our heads as our two legs.

Cats can survive falls no human could ever survive, because their inner ear mechanism enables them to detect the fall and turn themselves upright in midair. When the cat reaches the point of impact, the shock is spread over all four flexed limbs, distributing the force evenly. Cats can sometimes withstand a fall from great heights better than from a lower distance. The theory is that when a cat falls from a great height, its body forms a type of parachute.

The cat relaxes the muscles and essentially floats to the ground. The greater distance also gives the cat's internal mechanism time to right its position. Cats, even when falling from heights, don't often sustain serious injuries.

MORNING STIFFNESS

D o you ever get up in the morning feeling like the tin man on *The Wizard of Oz*—in need of an oil can? If you feel stiff and achy there is a strong chance you have a very common condition believed to be caused by lack of REM sleep.

If you are the parent of a baby, you might notice after a few nights of middle-of-the-night feedings or play sessions that you feel old and on the road to a major mid-life crisis. The problem is that you are sleeping but not reaching a state of deep relaxation.

When you are in a deep, stage four REM (Rapid Eye Movement) sleep, the brain is very active and your temperature and blood flow increases. This maintains your metabolism as you sleep.

When you are in non-REM sleep, your brain activity and metabolism slow down to their lowest levels. This causes the energy you need to keep your body running to also be at its lowest levels. If this continues without the interruption of the REM levels, your metabolism will be temporarily impaired. Your circulation will be sluggish and your internal temperature will drop, making you feel like you need a jump start in the morning.

People experiencing severe emotional stress will have the same problem with interrupted REM sleep. Their high anxiety levels will prevent full relaxation. This is why conditions such as fibrositis, characterized by this kind of morning muscle pain, are associated with stress.

Women are 80 percent more likely to have this condition, which is typically characterized by a pain that begins in the neck and continues down between the shoulder blades. Of course, women have been arguing for years that neck pain is caused by the men in their lives. This correlation is still under study.

Morning stiffness may also be caused by problems with neurotransmitters. There may be too much of what is called Substance P and too little serotonin. Serotonin disorders have been linked to sleep disturbances, increased pain perception, depression, and muscle spasms. One way to increase serotonin levels is through exercise. Also ask your doctor if any medications you may be taking interrupt REM sleep. If they do, ask for a medication substitute.

MOTION SICKNESS

Motion sickness represents one of the great ironies in life. To have motion sickness, our brain and sense of balance must be intact and working normally. In other words, sea, air, car, train, swing, and space sickness come to those of us who are neurologically healthy! This fact seems to rival the primary law of nature. What about "survival of the fittest"? If we're healthy, why do we get motion sickness? What's happening?

Not everyone is prone to motion sickness. Statistically, one in three adults is apt to suffer from it. Motion sickness is caused when our bodies experience repetitive angular and linear acceleration and deceleration. Simply speaking, a combination of movement in all directions—up and down, backwards and forwards, and side to side—that stops and starts is most likely to bring on motion sickness. Our bodies can usually handle a small dose of this movement, but an extended period of it does not allow our body to relax and say "uncle." In effect, motion sickness is the body's reaction to a motion overload.

Where does motion sickness get processed? In the ear. The ear not only hears but helps us keep our balance, too. A specialized system in our inner ear called the vestibular apparatus is responsible for coordinating our movements and keeping us from toppling over. Fluid-filled canals within the vestibular system, appropriately named the labyrinth because of their convoluted roller coaster design, are the main lines of balance communication with our brain. If the labyrinth experiences ordinary movement (walking and jumping), it can help us maintain our balance with amazing simplicity, accuracy, and precision. Precision is the key word. Our ability to balance ourselves is so well calibrated that our inner ear, acting as an organic level, has little tolerance for excessive stimulation. If we board a rocking and rolling, rising and dipping ship or sit in a jostling and jerking amusement ride, the fluids in our labyrinth become agitated; as the motion continues, they twirl and somersault wildly. Garbled messages emanate from this labyrinthine center and travel to our midbrain vomit center, to which our bodies respond with pallor, cold sweating, and rapid breathing. We inevitably reach for the "barf bag."

People often ask why everyone doesn't experience motion sickness. The answer is that, given enough time and stimulation, everyone would! Like with pain, we all have different levels of tolerance. Visual stimuli such as a moving horizon or printed page, poor ventilation and the presence of irritants such as cigarette and exhaust smoke, emotional conditions such as anxiety and fear, and even physical factors like a full stomach or the sight of food can precipitate an attack. Many amusement rides are deliberately designed to challenge our basic threshold for motion sickness—and we call them fun!

Motion sickness, like pregnancy, is an all or nothing phenomenon. Once you start the nausea and vomiting cycle, only time and removing the offending stimuli will help. In short, prevention is much easier than treatment. The primary nonmedical solution is learning how to use your eyes and how to hold your head still. We often hear the suggestion of focusing on a fixed object in times of heaving discomfort. In reality, the only object that doesn't appear

to move in these situations is the sky. So, when you begin to feel uncomfortable, focus your eyes on a point forty-five degrees above the horizon for relief.

Does closing our eyes help? For some people it can. If you can completely blank out your visual memory of moving objects prior to closing your eyes, then you will feel better. The problem is that most people can't make their mind a clear slate and therefore closing their eyes offers little help. So you might want to try closing your eyes once, but have a backup plan.

When all else fails, medication, from tablets to patches, should be taken before symptoms begin. Motion is in many ways like candy, too much of a good thing will make us ill.

NAUSEA AND VOMITING

Vomiting is the body's way of ridding itself of substances it can't digest. The most common cause of vomiting is just plain overindulgence in food, drink or both.

When you vomit, all of the muscles of the digestive tract—the stomach, esophagus, and cardiac sphincter—relax, while the muscles of the abdomen and diaphragm contract in powerful spasms. This squeezes the stomach and forces out whatever is inside. It is no wonder you feel exhausted and like your insides have been turned inside out after vomiting.

Nausea is that sickening feeling that comes before you vomit. Normally the stomach produces rhythmic contractions every twenty seconds or so to churn food and gastric juices. When the stomach is irritated by too much of something, it can become inflamed. This will cause a greater amount of churning, which can sometimes be forceful and debilitating. Nine times out of ten, vomiting will eliminate irritants and make you feel much better.

There is actually a vomit center in the brain stem that is activated when information is passed into it from the frontal lobes of the brain, the digestive tract, or the balancing mechanism in the inner ear. Once this happens, inevitably on a football Sunday or at college fraternities on Saturday night, it sends messages to the diaphragm that "you've overindulged," which puts in motion the process of vomiting.

Vomiting and nausea can be caused by emotional triggers such as studying for a final exam, hearing terrible news, or getting ready to walk down the aisle. When the body is faced with a stressful situation, it will respond as though it is under attack with an increase in the production of the hormones cortisol and epinephrine. This will lead to the elevation of the heart rate, blood pressure, and metabolic rate. These changes will stimulate the brain stem to activate the vomit center.

Nausea and vomiting are becoming common work-related maladies. According to the Environmental Protection Agency, many offices and buildings are more than one hundred times more polluted than the outside air. Chemicals, bacteria, and germs make the buildings virtually toxic for many workers, who then exhibit symptoms indicative of poor indoor air quality. So if you think work makes you sick to your stomach, pay attention. You may be right.

NUMBNESS

During our lives we face events that leave us speechless or dumfounded. We react with embarrassment when someone follows this spell with the question, "What's the matter with you?" Fortunately, our stranded thoughts are usually quickly ushered back into our dazed heads.

What happens? Why does the brain occasionally blank out, as if an eraser has wiped it clean, only to find an appropriate response seconds later? To answer this question, we must consider the type of stimulus that caused the blank-out and its timing.

Neurologically, several pathways found in the limbic system at the base of our brains help interconnect the events stored in our memories. Aside from helping link memories, the limbic area also controls most of our strong emotional responses. Usually the limbic system can juggle those two activities, but occasionally the brain can overload. Normally, if incoming stimuli trigger exceptionally strong emotions, a reflexive outpouring of nerve impulses bombards the limbic area, creating a smoke-screen effect. The limbic area is then unable to connect all immediate recall events—the present situation—with long term memory, the required response. This momentary delay is often colloquially referred to as "mental numbness." In medicine we call it benign forgetfulness. It's reassuring to know that this numbness bears no relationship to degenerative brain disorders or other types of chronic disease. A minor consolation for being called numb is the understanding that these sensations of cerebral emptiness are usually normal. Many of us use the expression "I can remember a face, but I just can't remember names." This phenomenon has little to do with benign forgetfulness and everything to do with concentration. Most psychological research proves that when we are initially introduced to someone we don't pay attention to their name. In effect, we can't forget something we didn't really learn. If you're a disbeliever, try recalling someone's name you met in passing today. Chances are, I gotcha!

Okay, but what about other types of numbness, the kind we feel in our arms or legs: Are they normal, too? No doubt you've heard of "Saturday Night Fever." It's a weekend dancing syndrome, where self-control for the week is unleashed and your body gyrates to pop music from dawn to dusk. But have you heard of "Saturday Night Palsy"? You may not know it by this name, but if you've gone to the movies and put your arm around your partner, you've certainly felt its symptoms. The nerves that innervate the sensory feelings and movement of our arm and hand travel on the underside of our axilla or armpit. This network of nerves is called the brachial plexus. When we wrap our arm around our sweetheart's shoulder (or, for the more timid, drape our arm along the top of their backrest), we inadvertently compress the nerves from our shoulder to the tip of our fingers. It takes no more than two to three minutes of this compression to develop a loss of sensation, or numbness, in the limb. Many believe that because the blood vessels are also squashed a tourniquet effect causes this numbness. In actuality, the loss of sensation first occurs because of a diminished transmission of sensory and motor impulses down the outside sheaths covering our nerves. Five to ten minutes later, the diminished blood supply to our arm also adds to our loss of feeling.

After we do lose feeling, what causes the characteristic sensa-

tion of pins and needles and the burning sensation called pares-
thesias? The answer has nothing to do with pin cushion mechanics
or changes in temperature. In order for our nerves to conduct
sensations, ions such as potassium, sodium, and chloride must pass
back and forth across our nerves' outer sheath. This constant movement helps set up the right environment for communication.
When our nerves are compressed, this ionic movement stops until
the pressure is released. Once the pressure is removed (by taking
your arm off your friend's shoulder), a sudden rush of ions bolts
across the nerve to resume the conduction process. This surge
mimics the sudden whiplash that occurs when firemen first turn
on a fire hose. The resulting sensation is a tingling or burning
feeling that subsides as soon as ionic equilibrium is reached (usually about one to two agonizing minutes later). It's interesting to
note that sitting on a chair without leg support or experiencing
vibration such as from a hairdryer, electric razor, or a steering
wheel in a car with unbalanced tires will give us the same risk of
"Saturday Night Palsy" as a good night at the movies.

In sum, transient nerve numbness, either mental or peripheral, is common. In fact, the next time you file out of a theatre
after seeing a blockbuster film, remember that one out of every
four couples (more if it's a romantic movie) is experiencing pins
and needles not induced by the movie plot.

ORGASM

An orgasm can be described as an intense explosion of energy. Your body throbs, you feel like you are going to burst with excitement, you feel tingly and may feel waves of pleasure from head to toe. For some people it produces a high similar to that caused by some mood-altering drugs.

When a person's brain receives messages of physical stimulation—sexy cologne or aftershave, a sensual body, a passionate kiss, a slow massage while you and your massager soak in a hot bathtub sprinkled with rose petals, surrounded by lighted candles and sipping Korbel Brut, or anything that will make you want to put this book down while you hunt for *your* spouse—the hypothalamus will release neurotransmitters which will signal bodily changes or signs of physical arousal.

For a man this physical arousal will cause the start of an erection. A woman will have some vaginal lubrication, a swelling of her clitoris and of the vaginal lips, which will also spread apart, nipple erection, and breast fullness. This is what Masters and Johnson would call the excitement phase of sexual response.

Then, as the man and woman start to act on their impulses, they move into the second phase, which Masters and Johnson call the plateau. Of course, it isn't easy for you to see these separate phases while you are in the middle of things, so don't be concerned if your lovemaking doesn't follow clear-cut delineations.

During the second phase the stimulation intensifies to prepare the body for orgasm. This is the time when you might be sweating, breathing heavily, and making funny animal noises.

At this point the male has a fully erect penis that is very warm with the end developing a reddish purple color. This is also the time when people have the most surprises. The man's Cowper's gland emits a few drops of semen-containing mucous, a phenomenon that is probably responsible for the conception of half of the human population.

At this phase the woman experiences swelling of the outer vagina and a closing of the vaginal opening. The inner vagina expands and the uterus raises higher. The clitoris becomes engorged and becomes hidden under the clitoral hood. Over 70 percent of women flush and may get a rash.

The next phase is many people's favorite: the orgasm. During phases one and two the body has become filled with a pleasant form of muscle tension or contraction called myotonia. As the stimulation continues both the man and woman may reach a point of pleasurable release when all the tension is discharged.

The man will have contractions of the muscles of the inner pelvis that massage the seminal fluid into the urethra from which it is then forcefully expelled.

When the woman reaches orgasm, the hypothalamus releases oxytocin, which will bring on irregular contractions of the voluntary muscles of the walls of the vagina and a release of tension in the pelvic area.

The great debate of the late twentieth century is whether or not a woman should have clitoral stimulation or vaginal stimulation in order to reach an orgasm. Not too long ago the great debate was whether or not a female could respond to sex at all.

In her book, *The Descent of Women,* Elaine Morgan describes the evolution of female responsiveness as being one of transition from our origins as quadrupeds to bipedalism. When we walked on all fours, there was no question that the female orgasm worked as well as could be designed. When the anatomy shifted and the vagina developed a "self-defeating curve where it bends around the pubic bone," orgasm for women became less efficient without some purposeful adjustments of position.

In other words, sexual pleasure for post-pliocene women requires some cooperation from their mates. Although it may still hold true in some societies, it was a prominent Victorian belief that women were not capable of any responsiveness at all. On their wedding day women were vaguely warned of something repulsive they would be forced to do on occasion to keep their husbands happy. Of course there is some evidence in Victorian literature that something was happening for women. In some graphic bedroom scenes heroines were described as applying "frenzied downward pressure on the hero's spine" as if to say "don't go—don't ever leave me." Right.

There is an assumption that animals do not experience anything like an orgasm because the mechanism in women is still undeveloped and in the throes of evolution, that it must have emerged first in homo sapiens, and because female quadrupeds walk away from copulation as if nothing happened.

Morgan claims that circumstantial evidence points to the fact that in the animal kingdom the sexual drive is a mutual affair. Both sexes feel a need and are compelled to satisfy it. There are no animals other than humans that can be mated against their will. Her conclusion is that orgasm is alive and well, only the animals do not make such a big deal about it.

PASSING GAS

A mericans are obsessed with flatulence, the fancy name for passing gas. If you listen to any six-year-old in the school yard, it is inevitable that you will hear the word "fart" at least once in the conversation, preferably within earshot of a horrified adult. When their children aren't around, adults do their share of giggling about gas. People still laugh uproariously over the classic scene of "beans around the campfire" in Mel Brook's seventies comedy *Blazing Saddles*.

Excess air that is not released by a burp usually goes into the intestines. There it is absorbed into the bloodstream and released either through the lungs or the rectum. Gas is also formed by the food we eat. There are certain types of foods, like beans, that contain substances that can not be completely digested. Beans have two nonabsorbable carbohydrates, raffinose and stachyose, that are fermented by bacteria that live in the colon. This produces gas. If you eat a lot of beans you will be grateful if you can pass the gas that is produced. Otherwise you will feel bloated, uncomfortable, and crampy. Some people actually have trouble passing gas. The gas actually forms a froth that gets stuck in the digestive tract. Mylanta, Riopan, and other over-the-counter remedies can help relieve the symptoms.

The infamous smell of gas depends on the type of food eaten and the microorganisms dominant in a person's bowel. The bac-

teria in the colon, which are beneficial to the body, feed on protein residue and form chemicals that, although present in small
amounts, pack a lot of power. If you are prone to a lot of gas, the
best way to avoid having to become a hermit is to eliminate certain

foods like dairy products (for those with lactose intolerance), spicy dishes, and carbonated beverages.

Those who like beans should know that they can be eaten without too much comedic effect if they are soaked overnight (discard the soaking water and add new water before cooking), are cooked for a long time or prepared with certain oriental seaweeds for increased digestibility. Bean products like tofu and tempeh are more digestible because they already have the carbohydrates broken down. Of course, for some people, the cure sounds worse than the cause.

PERSPIRATION

If you watch television for one hour, you will know without a doubt how Americans feel about sweat. At least according to Madison Avenue, if you are caught with body odor or telltale wetness, you may as well give up any illusions of being successful, desirable or marginally cool. Of course, that rule doesn't apply if you work out with the Soloflex or NordicTrack exercise machines. Their late night infomercials have elevated sweating to new heights of sex appeal.

Whether we like it or not, sweating serves an important function. Like a central cooling system for our bodies, it keeps our internal temperature separate from our outer environment. Humans are the only mammals with a cooling system that enables us to be efficient in hot weather. Most animals are lethargic in the heat because they rely on the insulation of their bodies and panting to keep them cool.

Human beings have what are called eccrine sweat glands that secrete water onto the skin in hot weather. When our temperature rises, the "sweat center" of the brain is signaled, which then triggers the eccrine glands to function. When these glands secrete water onto the skin in hot weather, it evaporates and we are cooled.

Human beings are the only creatures who purposely work harder in the heat for the fun of it. You don't see striped tigers hitting nine holes of golf or jogging ten miles for sport. With more exercise comes more sweating. An adult male exercising vigorously in the heat can lose up to two quarts of sweat in an hour. This can present a problem if there is too much water loss, because eventually you can't sweat enough to cool off. Your blood level will be too low and you will have lost valuable electrolytes. It is okay to exercise in the heat if you make sure to replenish fluids and if you become acclimated to the changes in temperature by increasing your exposure gradually. Your body needs time to adjust to the increased need for cooling.

By the way, sweating is not only caused by heat and exercise. In case you were wondering, you are not the only person in the world who can work up a sweat talking to your boss or filling out your tax return. Emotions play a large role in our sweat potential.

Some of the 3 million eccrine sweat glands located throughout our bodies are gathered in groups of three thousand per square inch on the palms of the hands, soles of the feet, and in the armpits. These glands respond to any kind of stress or emotion. This is not good news for those of us who believe you should "never let them see you sweat." In addition to the annoyance, this form of sweating seems to serve no function but for nearly one in ten of us embarrassment and high dry cleaning bills are the result.

As with many of our at first seemingly useless bodily functions, sweating may be a throwback to early evolution when we may have had to climb trees in a single leap to avoid a large, furry, ferocious creature. The increased moisture on the hands and feet could have made the difference between life and lunch.

Of course the eccrine glands under the arms would serve no purpose in that instance except to knock the predator over with an odoriferous frontal attack. Actually it is a misconception that sweat itself has an unpleasant odor. It is the bacteria working on the sweat that produces unlimited stock potential for underarm deodorant companies.

Under the arms, in the genital area, and around the nipples we also have what are called the apocrine glands. These glands are undeveloped in childhood but become activated during puberty. In times of stress and excitement they secrete a sticky, milky substance composed of proteins, carbohydrates, and lipids. This type of sweat is sterile and odorless until decomposed by bacteria. Then it takes on its unpleasant smell.

Maybe in cave days the smell wouldn't have been unpleasant. Theorists surmise that since odors function for animals as a chemical messenger to the opposite sex, maybe this form of sweating is the human way to subconsciously send sexual signals through the odor of chemicals known as pheromones.

This is only theory, and to date no pheromones have been detected in human sweat. So it is unlikely that we will be seeing a new set of men's and women's colognes called Essence of Body Odor any time soon.

REFLEXES

A reflex is an automatic reaction to a stimulus. It stems from the autonomic nervous system, which uses the brain stem and the hypothalamus to process information.

There are three basic types of reflexes: primitive, inborn, and conditioned. You can always tell a new parent from a seasoned one by how they respond to the primitive reflexes they see in their newborn.

I don't want to burst any balloons, but it is not a sign of genius when a newborn within the first two months looks like it is walking when you hold it upright. And do not count on a football scholarship based on the baby's grip. It is a primitive reflex to grasp any object placed in the baby's palm during the first four months of life. Other primitive reflexes are tonic neck, when the baby stretches its arms and legs out when it turns its head to one side; and Moro's reflex, where the baby swings its arms outward and then together in an embrace if its head is unsupported or if it is startled.

Perhaps the greatest relief for new mothers is the rooting reflex. When you rub a bottle nipple, breast, or finger on a baby's cheek near the corner of the mouth, it will turn its head so it can suck. The baby knows what to do even if the new mom is baffled. There is no question that the rooting reflex exists for the new baby's survival. Moro's reflex may have to do with keeping the baby balanced or protected.

Adults have inborn reflexes like babies do. You can test the condition of your nervous system by hitting your knee in the right spot. If the soles of your foot are irritated, your toes will curl, and your pupils will dilate in response to light.

Shivering when it is cold is an automatic reflex. We also have what is called the mammalian diving reflex, which switches the flow of blood from nonvital areas, such as hands and feet, and sends it to the heart, lungs, and brain if we suddenly find ourselves immersed in cold water. Drowning victims have been able to be revived after a full thirty minutes underwater because of this automatic response.

Conditioned reflexes are those automatic impulses that tell you your life is in a rut. When you are able to drive to work in a semicomatose state, you know that you have developed a conditioned reflex. And just try to move your wastebasket after it's been in the same place for twelve years. You are guaranteed to find wads of paper on the floor where the wastebasket used to be.

If we had to think about our reflexes before doing them, we would be in big trouble. Considering how long it takes for people to choose what movie to see, it is better that we are not given choices like whether or not to breathe.

Actually, breathing falls under a category of partially voluntary reflexes. We can control such things as breathing or emptying the bladder. But as any kindergartener will tell you, you can only hold either for so long.

RINGING IN THE EARS

One in six people in America have tinnitus, or "ringing in the ears," ranging from acute episodes to a chronic condition. Tinnitus is a Latin word literally meaning "to tinkle or ring like a bell." For those under its spell, tinnitus can mimic a constant ringing noise, sound like a swarm of cicadas on a warm summer day, or imitate the internal hum of a transformer tirelessly relaying annoying messages. Tinnitus can raise an individual's level of awareness so that they can hear themselves breathe, hear the internal movement of their joints, and even hear the constant thump of their pulse. These internal noises range from mild levels to intensities so severe that the inflicted person might think he or she is going mad. The origins of the problem range from inspissated cerumen (dried earwax plugging the auditory canal) to an acoustic tumor or the most common drug-related cause, the overuse of aspirin (salicylic acid).

The most common nondrug cause of ringing in the ears is overexposure to loud noises. A visit to a rock concert is a quick reminder that exposure to loud music is the main cause of tinnitus in people under thirty. However, any exposure to loud noise can cause the problem. Impact noise, such as gunshots, or chronic noise, such as chain saws, loud machinery, lawn mowers, and the common bathroom culprit—hair dryers—can all put a strain on our internal hearing.

A commonly asked question is, what constitutes loud noise? The answer is a simple one. You don't need to memorize decibels or acoustic statistics. If you cannot hear normal conversation from four feet away, the noise is too loud and/or your hearing is impaired.

Understanding ear anatomy will help you to appreciate ringing in the ears. Our ear has three functional parts. The outer ear acts as a funnel for sound. The middle ear acts as an interpreter and changes sound into mechanical energy by vibrating the eardrum and transferring this energy through little bones called the anvil, stirrup, and hammer to the inner ear. There are microscopic hairs on the auditory cells in the inner ear. When the ear is healthy and experiencing normal exposure to sound waves, the hairs move in balance with the mechanical pressure exerted by the sounds that vibrate the eardrum. This hair movement is associated with a chemical change that ultimately sends electrical impulses to the brain through the cochlea, the snail-like fluid-filled compartment in the inner ear. These hairs can be damaged and literally immobilized through repeated exposure to loud noise, thus rendering them useless as part of the sound relay team to the brain. This damage, however, does not necessarily mean that there will be measurable hearing loss. It does mean, though, that extraneous noise such as a ringing of the ear may be introduced into the hearing process.

While ringing of the ear due to inner ear damage is frequently not reversible, there are several forms of treatment. One that has gained approval by the Food and Drug Administration is the use of an electronic noise source called a masker. The device is similar in physical appearance to a hearing aid and works by actually replacing the ringing with another sound that tends to cancel the internal noise by overriding it with an external one. A similar principle is used when music is played in an office to mask the routine sounds of ventilator fans or computer noise. The masking unit is placed inside the ear, and with current technology it can actually be almost out of view of the external world. Masking devices require FDA approval, however, since they may become too much of a good thing due to their potential risk of inadvertently producing masking noises that in themselves may be too loud for our own good.

RUNNER'S HIGH

Have you ever been sitting on a park bench eating an ice-cream with your "spare tire" hanging over your belt when a muscle-faced jogger came running by?

As you hyperventilate climbing up the seven steps to your office, do you ever wonder what they see in all that exercise? Did you know that while you have to drink at least two beers to get even a slight buzz, they may be reaching a high one hundred times more potent than morphine? Legally?

The existence of a "runner's high" or "exercise-induced euphoria" was discovered in the mid-seventies. Medical professionals determined that people who exercise vigorously for as little as twelve minutes produce beta-endorphins, a natural painkiller, that can heighten their sense of well-being.

Endorphins are neurotransmitters, molecules that transmit information between and among the brain cells. There are over 100 billion brain cells (neurons), which are linked by the neurotransmitters into a complex network. The neurons fire electrochemical impulses at different rates to trigger the release of neurotransmitters, which then cause other nerve cells to fire. When all of these reactions work in harmony with each other, specific biochemical messages are sent to the brain to tell us to perform certain tasks, such as thinking and talking.

A good sweat can also produce the chemical norepinephrine,

which has been known to improve moods. Norepinephrine is a chemical made in the adrenal glands and found in the brain that acts on the entire body in times of stress to speed up the heart rate, restrict blood vessels, and put the body in a state of high alert.

You can achieve the exercise-induced euphoric feeling from many activities other than running, including walking at a brisk pace. However, you need to do the activity vigorously for at least twelve minutes to feel any of the effects.

The longer you run, the more tired you feel. However, there is a certain point at which you can burst through a type of "wall" into a state of euphoria. You experience a second wind or renewed burst of energy and feel like you can keep on running indefinitely.

Studies have shown an increased level of beta-endorphins in the bloodstream of people doing sustained levels of exercise. Beta-endorphins are also found throughout the body at various opiate receptor sites. Although running for an hour or more might pro-

duce a runner's high, this is probably a side effect of the body's effort to cope with such a high level of stress.

The human body was not originally designed to run marathons for sport. We were designed, however, to be able to run in short bursts to escape wild animals or enraged rivals wielding heavy clubs. With norepinephrine and beta-endorphin the body can perform extraordinary feats when necessary. The runner's high is the body's way of accommodating the abnormal conditions of sustained stressful activity while still maintaining some kind of internal balance.

There have always been exercise pioneers advocating exertion as the road to health. Perhaps the most interesting commentary about human nature is that the discovery of the direct exercise, beta-endorphin, and euphoria connection lead to the unprecedented development of a large population who see fitness as a side effect of feeling good.

RUNNY NOSE

hildren and runny noses go together. A runny nose will not bother a two-year-old who might improvise with a quick wipe of a sleeve, but to a mother they are a symbol that she is not doing her job. No matter how hard she tries, however, most children will bring home six to twelve colds a year when they hit school age. They are exposed to all kinds of new viruses for which they have not developed immunity.

Nasal discharge is caused by inflammation of the mucous lining of the nose. Most people like to dry it up with over-the-counter medication, which is fine in moderation, but some people believe it is best to let it run its course. If you swallow the mucous, which sounds yucky, but is what most of us do when we sniffle, you prolong the symptoms and draw the mucous back into your chest. The best way to handle a runny nose is to blow it gently, relax, and wait for it to dry up on its own.

There is little truth to the rumor that colds are spread by kissing. Studies have shown that enzymes in saliva might actually help destroy cold viruses. You spread colds more easily by shaking hands than by planting a wet one.

It is also a myth that you can get a cold by standing out in bad weather. If you have the rhinovirus in your body prior to exposure, you may exacerbate the symptoms, but you stand a better chance of developing a cold indoors. Dry environments like our typical homes dry up the mucous membranes in the nose making them more susceptible to virus attack.

Some recent studies have shown that capsaicin, the ingredient found in chili peppers, can have a positive effect on stuffy noses. The only problem is that you do not take it internally, you have to put it directly into your nose. Although stuffy noses are red anyway, you might feel a bit conspicuous doing this.

SEEING STARS

There is something very special about the celestial bodies we call stars. We place their likeness on our preschoolers' foreheads. We compare our favorite television movie, and sports personalities to their brilliance. We even measure the enthusiasm we imagine in a child's mind by "seeing stars in their eyes." But apart from what we see in others, there is also what we see through our own shut eyes that look like the stars we admire. What is this sensation we call "seeing stars," and when does it most commonly happen?

First, let's agree that, as with viewing any object, what we describe as "seeing stars" depends on our individual perception. As such, the term is frequently overused. Many of us link seeing stars with common visual disturbances such as dizziness or blurred vision. These conditions often cause us to temporarily view the world as a mass of twinkling lights magnified through water droplets or flakes of melting snow. But this visual experience is only half of the story. The true definition of "seeing stars" requires not just the projection of a heavenly kaleidoscope on the backside of our eyelid, but also an accompanying feeling of angelic levitation, a magic carpet ride.

Seeing stars happens when we are at the brink of losing our consciousness. Normally we "take" a picture similarly to the way a camera does. Our eye is the lens. Our iris is the aperture. Our retina is the film. From the retina, the optic nerve carries the information to our visual cortex, called the occipital lobe. The occipital lobe is about the size of a plum and is found at the rear of our brain. Just as a camera has an on/off switch, so does our visual brain. Our "arousal button" is a clump of cells in our brain stem named the reticular formation (RF). When we get a good bump on our head, receive anesthesia, hold our breath, get drunk, have a high fever, or hyperventilate, the pathway from our reticular formation to our occipital lobe becomes agitated. The result is akin to us turning a television set on or off. At the specific moment we click our tuner and affect the power supply we see a "flash surge" and a faint picture roll. A similar phenomenon occurs when we interrupt our full consciousness (RF). The flash surge and feeling of weaving we sense is called "seeing stars." Once the interrupting stimuli is removed or our visual pathways have time to adjust, the mental celestial bodies we see fade away, and real images replace them.

Do headaches and fluorescent lights have anything to do with seeing stars? For those of us who experience migraines or have had a focal epileptic seizure, the answer is yes.

A classic migraine has, as part of its syndrome, a twenty to thirty minute prodrome (period before the headache) of visual disturbances that include scintillating zigzig lines and flashes of light. This "aura" is particularly vivid since the trigeminal nerve pathway involved in the migraine process runs reasonably close to our reticular formation. The constant stimulation of both decreased blood flow and increased nerve involvement associated with the migraine process causes us to "see stars."

Although the aura in migraines may seem reasonable, what is the connection with fluorescent light bulbs? Well, fresh fluorescent lights, when working normally, are of no real consequence to us. They usually work at sixty cycles per second, and physiologically are imperceptible. However, when a fluorescent bulb nears the end of its life, it can pulse as low as ten cycles per second. This flicker frequency is not only noticeable to our eye, but the stimulus can interrupt the pathway traveling from the visual cortex to the arousal center. If disruption does occur, we call the resulting "seeing stars" a visual focal seizure. Anxiety-provoking but not dangerous, approximately one in two hundred adults are candidates for seeing stars from fading fluorescent light bulbs.

For many of us, the closest we'll ever get to seeing stars is gazing up into the nighttime sky. For others, we'll catch a celebrity dining at a local restaurant, and for a few of us, we'll see stars in our own private screening room behind our eyelids.

SHINSPLINTS

To the weekend warrior, the over-thirty armchair athletes who every so often have the urge to go for the burn, even the word shinsplints is painful.

"Shinsplints" is actually a generic term for chronic exercise-induced leg pain. It affects the lower leg and may be caused by chronic compartment syndrome, where there is a buildup of pressure in a leg muscle as a result of exercise; inflammation of a tendon; nerve entrapment on the side of the calf; inflammation of a muscle; or inflammation of the membrane over the bone.

No matter how it is caused, it can range from a dull pain that is barely noticeable to a stiffness that makes you look like a candidate for social security. If you exercise through the pain, which is not smart unless you are trying to impress someone who's really worth it, you could wind up needing drug treatment or surgery. The best thing to do when you get shinsplints is to use them as an excuse to rest it out for a week or two.

You can get shinsplints from standing on a hard floor for long periods of time or from wearing high heels. Since this can't always be avoided in certain jobs or situations, it is a good idea to wear shoes with good arch support and to do leg-stretching exercises whenever possible.

People with flat feet run a greater risk of getting shinsplints, because arches make good shock absorbers. Fortunately for flat-footed athletes, orthopedic shoes no longer make you look like Dr. Frankenstein's monster's cousin. There are also so many different styles of athletic shoes that it would be impossible not to find one to at least offset the problem.

If you decide after your next once-a-year workout that you don't want to ever do that to yourself again, you may want to consider a regular low-impact exercise routine. Low impact routines such as the Diet Workshop's "Lighten Up" have been proven to be as effective as high-impact routines, with fewer injuries. This doesn't mean remote control aerobics. Low impact can mean anything from brisk walking to bike riding to dance. Twenty minutes three times a week can make the difference.

SKIN SHRIVELING IN WATER

The evidence seems so clear. If I add water to rice, it puffs up. If I use a paper towel to clean up a water spill, it absorbs, and a sponge, well, everyone knows that sponges expand as soon as they come close to water. So why in the world have I known since I was a toddler that if I stay in a bathtub too long my fingers and toes will shrivel and look like a bunch of prunes?

The answer lies in one major difference between our skin and a paper towel or a sponge. Our skin is designed to protect us by keeping substances out. Towels and sponges are designed to take substances in.

The best demonstration of the normal role of our skin as a protective organ actually comes after we get our Kodak prints back from developing. If we do not carefully hold the edges as we take the prints out of the envelope, we soon see our developed pictures through a film of greasy fingerprints. These same oils that ruin pictures naturally combine with the outermost keratinized layer of our skin (made up of nonliving waterproof cells). This dynamic duo works to our advantage by protecting us from harmful bacteria and toxic substances in our external environment. It is these very same protective elements that we hamper when our skin becomes shriveled in water.

So, how does skin transform itself from the largest protective organ in our body to a shriveled prune? The answer is found when we examine what happens when we remove the protective barriers on our skin.

Two of the worst enemies our skin could encounter in the bathtub are soap and the hard minerals that naturally are found in water. When we take a bath, both of these villians work together to remove the oils from the palms of our hands and the soles of our feet. As the oils are removed, the tough keratinized layer of our skin called the stratum corneum is softened and loosened, becoming penetrable to water. Once our toe hits the H_2O, the initial signs of dimpling begin, and identifiable shriveling takes place about fifteen minutes later. An interesting note here is that if you have ever used paint thinner or nail-polish remover and accidentally spilled some on your hands, the above fifteen minute rule is off! These agents are such powerful detergents (oil removers) that skin shriveling occurs in a matter of seconds, not minutes.

You're saying, I still don't get it. My skin is usually protected, soap and minerals dissolve this protection, but why the shriveling? Why don't I swell like a sponge instead? It's a thoughtful question, yet one that has a straightforward answer. At the outset, we need to know that without protection our hands and feet become *dehydrated* in the presence of water, not hydrated. It works this way. Around 75 percent of our body is water. This amount varies depending on the amount of fat we have. Dehydration happens when the protective film on our skin surface is lost and our body water begins to leak out of our skin cells. These cells have semipermeable membranes in their walls. This means that they can give up water, but they can't take it in as easily. Following this principle, once the protective layer on our skin is lost, the flood gates open outward, the water moves out, and shriveling becomes an inevitability.

Here's an interesting piece of trivia regarding skin shriveling in the presence of water. Have you noticed that when the skin on your hands or feet shrivels, it's usually the palms and soles that are affected, while the backs of your hands and the arches of your feet are spared? This occurs because the backs of our hands and arches of our feet have sebaceous glands that continually replenish protective oils as the water we are immersed in takes them away. Unfortunately, our soles and palms are more susceptible to shriveling, but fortunately this also means they are less likely to leave major grease spots on fine stationery.

SNEEZING

In the movie *My Stepmother Is an Alien,* Kim Basinger, whose character is experiencing human form for the first time, describes that one of the most pleasurable aspects of being human is our ability to sneeze.

Sneezes can be annoying when they accompany head colds or appear at inopportune times, but they do produce a feeling of relief that is kind of nice. This is especially evident when a sneeze gets stuck in your nose. You feel it coming on, you inhale deeply and wait for it, but it fizzles out. Yet you still feel a stuffy sense or an itch that is just begging to be relieved. A sneeze that follows a false alarm is a pleasure unto itself.

Usually sneezes work themselves out on their own. But a really stubborn sneeze can be encouraged by sniffing a bit of pepper. Interestingly, Victorian gentlemen inhaled pinches of snuff—powdered tobacco—to make themselves sneeze for pleasurable reasons. They did it because the nose has capillary sinusoids similar to those found in the penis. The inflow and outflow of blood in these capillary sinusoids (blood vessel beds) gives an individual a sudden rush of euphoria. Nasal tissue is often referred to as erectile tissue, which is why some men have sneezing fits during intercourse.

A sneeze is like an explosion emanating from your nose. It can expel air at speeds of one hundred or more miles per hour. Each sneeze contains up to five thousand droplets of mucous-filled air and can travel up to twelve feet.

It is customary to say something when someone sneezes. This tradition has its roots in many cultures. The Jewish custom is for the person who sneezes to say something instead of waiting for a chorus of "God bless you." According to legend there was a time in the history of the world when no one was ever sick. When the time of death approached, the otherwise healthy person would sneeze and the soul would leave the body through the nose. Therefore when Jacob, the Jewish patriarch, began to sneeze while blessing his sons, he knew his death was near. He prayed to God to allow him to live long enough to bless all his sons, which is why, according to Jewish custom, that when you sneeze you should thank God that you are still alive.

The standard variation of this legend is that the soul leaves the body during a sneeze, so if others do not shout "God bless you," devils may invade. Some people attribute the saying of "God bless you" after a sneeze to Pope Gregory the Great who is said to have originated it during an outbreak of bubonic plague during the sixth century. Water droplets from sneezing were a common medium of the disease's transmission.

Run-of-the mill sneezes are a protective response to irritant particles settling on the sensitive mucous membranes inside the nose. They are also caused by inflammation of the upper respiratory tract due to a cold, flu or hay fever.

When the membranes are irritated, they send messages to the respiratory center located at the base of the brain. The signals are then sent instantaneously to the muscles associated with breathing. This causes you to inhale and then to close the airways while using the respiratory muscles to squeeze the chest. Consequently, the air pressure in the lungs is raised. When the pressure reaches a certain point, the airways open and the air is expelled along with any foreign particles or irritants.

Since most of us do not see the pleasure associated with runny, drippy sneezes during cold season, we usually take any number of remedies to arrest the symptoms. This is not always the best idea, because the internal cleansing that occurs with sneezing can often hasten our recovery.

Sneeze bashing is not a phenomenon of modern society. Folk remedies for the dreaded sneeze abound, including pressing on the upper lip, rubbing the face, wrist, and ankles with lard, and sniffing garlic, witch hazel, horseradish, alcohol, or olive oil.

SNORING

Sawing a few logs" (snoring) during the night may not bother you very much, since most snorers don't even know they are doing it, but don't be surprised if you wake up one morning with your spouse poised to strangle you. Some snores—those raspy, gaspy, whistling noises emanating from a happily sleeping person—can reach eighty decibels. That is like the sound of a diesel engine when you are sitting in the back of a bus. In general, men are more likely to snore than women, and obese people are much more likely to snore than those who are not obese.

In England a couple actually sued their neighbor for keeping them up at night with her snoring. Basil and Sandra Davies sought a noise abatement ban on Mrs. Florrie Phillips, claiming her snoring not only kept them up but gave Mr. Davies angina attacks. They reached a compromise that included several forms of soundproofing. A spokesperson for the Noise Abatement Society said the snoring was louder than the legal limit set in England for motorcycles.

Aside from soundproofing, Mrs. Phillips could have considered some of the innumerable patented gadgets and folk remedies

to stop her snoring. For example, she could strap herself to her bed to avoid moving while she slept, although there is no proof this does anything to stop snoring. Or she could use a snore alarm to alert her to her snoring, but this probably only serves the purpose of making the snorer as miserable as his or her victims.

She could have sewn a button or taped a tennis ball or marble to the back of her pajamas to keep her from sleeping on her back. This "cure" may be somewhat effective, because snoring is often caused by poor muscle tone in the pharynx, palate, and tongue. This causes the airway tube to collapse into itself much like the neck of a balloon collapsing. The noise is caused by a vibration in the soft palate while the lungs work extra hard to draw in air through the partially blocked passageway. Sleeping on the stomach may actually work to keep the airways from collapsing into themselves. However, if the muscle tone is in good shape, sleeping on your back can cause the tongue to fall backward in the throat, partially closing the airway.

Other causes of snoring are nasal deformities, enlarged tonsils or adenoids, nasal allergies, heavy smoking, consuming gluttonous amounts of food before bedtime, and heavy consumption of alcohol. Tranquilizers and antihistamines can relax the muscles in the air passage and also cause snoring.

Although snoring is not usually considered more than grounds for divorce or justifiable homicide, there are cases where it is an indication of a more serious condition called sleep apnea. This is where the air passages are completely obstructed several times during the night. Once it is determined by sleep studies that this is the problem, it can be eliminated through surgery or the use of a pressurized mask worn during the night.

Although sleep apnea should be evaluated, snoring itself is not usually life threatening, even though exasperated spouses might consider snore prevention gadgets to maintain their own sense of well-being.

STITCH

Astitch is a pain that can literally take your breath away. It feels like a sharp stab in the upper part of the abdomen, between the ribs and the stomach, and is caused by a cramping of the diaphragm. Although we may not admit it, when we get a stitch we most probably assume the worst. There are many causes of this type of spasm, none of which are life threatening.

If you are an athlete, you might get a stitch because of gas formed by the digestion of food. Exercise speeds up intestinal contractions and will push the gas already in your colon to the rectum. If you do not find a way to expel it, which can be a bit embarrassing in front of a close crowd, you may get a stitch.

The diaphragm will cramp if it has pressure from the lungs above and the abdomen below. If you breathe hard, like when you are running, your lungs will fill up with air and push down on your diaphragm. When you run, you also lift your legs up with each step, which means you must contract your stomach muscles. This exerts pressure from below on the diaphragm. The pressure from both directions closes off the blood supply and causes the stitch.

Food sensitivities can make you prone to getting a stitch after exercise. Some people who are allergic to wheat or milk and lack the enzymes to break them down in their intestines may get a stitch if they exercise within twenty-four hours of eating those foods.

When we grow up, we want to do everything our mothers told

us not to do. Drink out of the juice carton if you want to, but do not go swimming within an hour after eating. As much as we hate to admit it, our mothers were right. Digestion takes energy, swimming takes energy, and the cold water puts a strain on your circulatory system. The combination is likely to cause a cramp if you swim within an hour after eating.

STUTTERING

lthough Porky Pig is most famous for it, over 2.5 million Americans stutter.

There are many theories about the causes of stuttering, some of which date back thousands of years. The Romans believed stutterers were possessed by evil spirits. In medieval times it was believed the tongue of the stutterer was evil in itself. Hippocrates thought stuttering was caused by a dry tongue, and a nineteenth century Prussian surgeon concluded stutterers' tongues were too large for their mouths.

Stuttering myths still prevail today. The general population believes stuttering is simply a psychological problem. While it is true that many people who stutter have emotional problems, these are sometimes the result rather than the cause of their stutter. As one stutterer remarked to his speech teacher, probably after a series of overly probing questions: "I am bugged because my speech is plugged."

Another common myth is that stutterers are somehow mentally deficient. Many well-meaning listeners will fill in the words for stutterers, thinking lack of vocabulary is to blame. This is almost as silly to watch as someone who shouts at a non-English speaking person or tries to imitate their accent so they can understand better.

The fact is, stutterers tend to have above normal IQ levels, averaging 14 percent higher than the general population. The locking of the vocal chords, the main mechanism of stuttering, has little to do with what is actually being said except to the extent that the flow or lack of flow of air creates the conditions for stuttering.

Stutterers all fall within the 2.5 percent of the population of people who have stress-induced muscle tension areas in their vocal chords. Everyone has some kind of muscle tension induced by stress, but the three main areas are the abdominal wall, the back of the neck, and the face. There is a smaller group, the 2.5 percent, who have their muscle tension in their vocal chords in the throat behind the Adam's apple. In conditions of stress this 2.5 percent of the population will focus the stress on their vocal chords.

Not all of these people stutter, but all stutterers come from this population. There are over five times as many males who stutter than females, which may have something to do with the structure of the throat and the prominence of the Adam's apple in men.

Although many men have been known to stutter only when uttering the "L" or "M" sounds, rarely does one become a stutterer as an adult without having stuttered as a child. Some people seem to outgrow stuttering, but if the conditions are right, unless new coping mechanisms are learned, stuttering can return.

Some researchers have found neurological connections to stuttering. Tests have shown irregularities in the part of the brain that controls the larynx as well as other subtle irregularities in the electrical activity and blood flow of 60 percent of the stutterers.

Neurological studies have confirmed that stuttering improves when the speaker is relaxed and not under pressure to talk. Oddly enough, stutterers do not stutter when they sing or when they talk to animals. This may be because singing uses a different part of the brain than speaking, and animals are more likely to be accepting and patient.

Stuttering is actually a learned behavior. While stutterers have the predisposition to vocal tension, the stutter is caused by the struggle to unlock the vocal chords. Between the ages of two and six, a child who has vocal tension and is experiencing the stress of learning how to talk may have a locking of the vocal chords. This is much like an elevator that gets stuck between floors. If you have ever been stuck in an elevator, particularly if it is with someone who looks like Charles Manson, you know that the first impulse is to pound all of the buttons to try to get the elevator to move.

When a child has locked vocal chords, he will naturally struggle to get them to unlock. The struggle becomes the conditioned reflex or a habit that we know as a stutter. As the child grows, whenever he feels tension on the vocal chords he will automatically stutter to avoid locking up.

A lot of times a child will realize that certain words or sounds, particularly those that originate in the front of the mouth and require no passage of air, cause locking. He will then avoid them altogether by word substitution. This is not a cure for stuttering and probably requires much more energy than learning to manage vocal stress.

SUNBURN

No one has to tell you when you have a sunburn. All they have to do is touch you. After you're scraped off the ceiling, you may start to notice other signs of sunburn such as tightness (due to skin dehydration) and pain every time you try to move.

There is no way to feel comfortable when you have a sunburn. You'll even have trouble wearing your clothing. If you try walking around without any apparel on, you'll find that even a wisp of air rubbing against you will cause you to want to jump right out of your skin. Cold compresses help deaden the pain by slowing down the conduction of the nerves feeding the inflamed area. Aspirin and other analgesics dull the throbbing as well by blocking pain chemicals like prostaglandins. Some people use aloe gel or a topical anesthetic like lidocaine or Xylocaine for relief. Above all, time is the best healer.

Sunburn is caused by the sun's ultraviolet rays, which penetrate our outermost dead skin layer, the stratum corneum (most of us know it as the layer that combines with dissolved soap to make the "ring around the bathtub"), and enter the outermost bloodless first living layer of our skin, the epidermis. The sun's rays complete their journey by entering our next layer, the dermis, which contains our skin's blood supply.

When ultraviolet A and B rays penetrate our epidermal and

dermal layers, they kill a large number of cells along the way (it is a myth that only B rays "burn"—they both do). In response, our white blood cells leave the dermal layer and travel back up to and infiltrate the epidermis to form a protective blister. A common sunburn question is, Do I break the blisters? The answer is no. Blisters are guarding what's left of your damaged skin. Unless blisters are in an area, such as a joint, where friction will eventually break them, they should be left alone. Sunburn care requires patience. Although it only takes fifteen to twenty minutes to get a sunburn, it takes about four days for the redness and the fluid beneath the blister to be reabsorbed and for all the cells to be shed as scales. We know this process as the postsunburn peel.

That cells die with sun exposure is understandable, but why does it appear that our blood flows nearer to the surface of our skin when we get sunburned? First, our blood does flow nearer to the surface of our skin by at least the width of heavy bond paper. Sunburn and long-term exposure to the sun causes dramatic thinning of the epidermis. Biopsy tests have shown that the epidermis, when damaged, will change from a very youthful twenty layers deep to a tissue-paper-thin two to three cells deep. This destruction is coupled with a reflexive engorgement of the blood vessels in the underlying dermal layer, which causes our blood to flow nearer to the surface of our skin, leading to increased redness, bruising, and infection.

When our skin is exposed to sun damage, our skin pigment (coloration) is dramatically changed. Hundreds of people walking around us are living testimony to this fact as they grow older and "actinic keratosis," or pigmented lesions appear on their skin. Like our brain, our skin cells have a superb memory, and accumulate and tabulate the stress of careless skin protection with the precision of a trained accountant. Chronic sun damage creates piles of pigment beneath our epidermis. These mounds are trans-

lated onto our legs, arms, neck, and face as unattractive sun freckles. These freckles occur because pigment-producing cells called
melanocytes become extremely active and subsequently release
melanin unevenly into our skin.

Does everyone tan, even dark-skinned people? The answer is
yes, but the degree of tanning varies from person to person. Well
then, what is a tan? Skin tans result from the homogeneous production of pigment from melanocytes, nature's skin painters in
our body. A little-known fact is that there are really two different
types of tan, immediate and delayed. Immediate tanning occurs
through ordinary window glass or under direct sunlight. It is a
result of ultraviolet exposure to precursors of melanin present in
our cells. Since these precursors in our skin are very limited, immediate tanning is a very subtle process and gives us a light bronze
glow when exposed. Delayed tanning, the type we usually refer to
as a tan, begins about ten hours after a sunburn and reaches a peak
about four to seven days later. A delayed tan fades gradually as we

shed activated pigmented cells. Within thirty days a tan is gone, even from the most fervent of vacationers, unless it is renewed with more time in the sun.

How much acquired tan is good for our skin? The American Academy of Dermatology says none and strongly endorses the use of sun-blocking creams. We once felt reassured that we could avoid sunburn by staying out of the sun between eleven A.M. and three P.M.. But this time window is now considered inaccurate, since it does not account for seasonal changes and geographical locations. A new rule of thumb, developed by meteorologist astronomer Leith Holloway, called the shadow method has come into favor. Holloway states that we can always determine when to get out of the sun by monitoring when our shadow is shorter than our height.

This simple rule may not be so simple for people who have difficulty "eyeballing" measurements. So to be truly accurate, you can consider that six of your foot lengths placed end to end will equal your approximate height. If your shadow's length is less than this measurement beware of the ill effects of the sun and cover up appropriately.

SWELLING FEET

sk any pregnant woman about swollen feet and you will
get a definite look of disgust. Swollen bellies are cute and
can be covered with T-shirts that say BABY ON BOARD. But
swollen feet that resemble ham hocks, aside from making you feel
unattractive, can be more uncomfortable than many of the other
common ailments that come with pregnancy. Swollen feet are not
the private domain of moms-in-the-making, however. Anyone who
is alive, stands up, crosses their legs, or wears shoes, can develop
swollen feet.

The veins in our lower legs are like the valves on a kitchen
faucet. They have tiny gates that regulate the stream of blood back
to our heart like a faucet controls water flow into the sink. The
process works against gravity with the help of body movement and
the position of our legs.

If we stand or sit for long periods of time or cross our legs
excessively, the process of circulation will be outweighed by the
gravitational pull. What goes down stays down. The fluid, instead
of fully circulating, will pool in our feet, ankles, and toes.

When you put your shoes on in the morning, everything appears fine. But if the fluid is pooling, the shoes act as a dam to hold
the waters back. If you take off your shoes, watch out. Once the
floodgates are opened, the feet will swell up like ripe tomatoes.

Don't worry, they won't explode. After a few minutes the

movement of your body will recirculate the blood and eventually restore your feet to their former beautiful selves.

Whenever possible put your feet up on a stool while watching TV. When on a long airplane flight, move about. These actions aren't bad manners, they are good preventive measures against swelling feet!

TASTE

We all link our tongue with our sensation of taste, but few stop to ponder the incredible versatility of this organ, which weighs about four ounces (only twice the weight of a U.S. Post Office express mail envelope). It helps us whistle, speak, measure the size of a cavity, demonstrate our displeasure or pleasure, and most of all helps us savor the calories we need to keep our body running.

Our tongue has approximately ten thousand taste buds on its surface. Although it may seem like a lot, this is actually dramatically fewer than the number we had when we were children. As babies, our taste buds were not only on our tongue, but were also nearly everywhere else in our mouth. The abundant supply of taste buds babies' mouths have throughout infancy is nature's way of insuring that we eat and thrive. As we grow older, our learned behavior and growing supply of remembered taste experiences allow us to enjoy a multitude of flavors with fewer taste buds.

As adults, each remaining taste bud is assigned only one of four primary functions, the identification of either salt, sweet, sour or bitter tastes of food as it passes over our tongue. Our brain coordinates these primary groups so that they work together in unraveling the myriad of possible flavor combinations found in our daily diet. Modern marketing promotions like the Pepsi/Coke challenge demonstrate the ability of our tongue to discern the difference between very similar tastes. Yet taste testing is not a new activity. For centuries, monks used their palates and noses extensively to perfect the flavors of fermented earthly "spirits" that they made from grapes grown in their abbey vineyards. Historians also note that ancient Greek sailors could tell where a fish had been caught simply by how it tasted!

This ability that our tongue has to identify thousands of individual foods and their combinations is extraordinary. How does it establish a memory of every flavor we eat from four simple tastes? Well, the location of taste buds and their assigned function are part of the answer. Our tongue is organized into zones for specific tasting roles. The tip of our tongue is sensitive to sweetness. It's for this reason that licking an ice cream cone or the baking spoon is an absolute treat. Conversely, the back of our tongue is the designated area for bitterness. It's because of this that we often take a spoonful of medicine with a water chaser. If we are quick enough, the bitter drug we must swallow will pass through our mouth thankfully unrecognized. Those who've let an aspirin sit too long on their tongue know just how alert those bitter buds are and have the bitter incentive needed to swallow with more alacrity the next time around.

Something bitter, like the first sip of a cup of coffee, can cause us to gag sometimes, even if we usually enjoy the bitter flavor. This is a reflex that becomes activated if too much of a bitter thing hits the back of our tongue and shocks the bitter-sensitive taste buds. If this happens to you, remain calm; although it may come at an embarrassing moment (in a restaurant), remember, it's usually normal. While we're on the topic of bitterness and tongues, have you ever wondered why when we do taste a bitter food like a lemon, we immediately stick out our tongue? The answer is not, as many would guess, that we're trying to spit out the taste, but rather that we've learned unconsciously from past experience (babies don't stick out their tongues) that air makes the taste more palatable. This spontaneous neutralization occurs because the chemicals causing the bitterness are broken down (oxidized) in the presence of oxygen.

An interesting aside here. Chances are you've occasionally had a pill stick in your throat when you've tried to beat its bitter taste with just a sip of water. What happens here is that the pill that you took landed on an anatomical shelf located between your voice box (larynx) and the upper part of your throat called the piriform recess. To avoid this problem in the future, simply take the time to drink a full glass of water with medication instead of taking only a few swigs.

While the tip and back of our tongue sense sweet and bitter tastes, salt and sour receptors line the edges of our tongue. This is the primary reason why canker sores, principally associated with overexposure to salty or sour foods, are also found at the edge of our tongue.

Well, that covers the tongue, but there's another tasting organ

in our body. One sensor is our tongue, and the other is our nose! As unbelievable as it may sound, of the two, our nostrils are significantly more sensitive—1000 times more sensitive to be exact—to flavor than our taste buds. Why is this the case? It's simply an issue of proper priming. In order for our tongue's taste buds to work as receptors, they must initially become "wetted" by saliva. No saliva, no taste! In contrast, the olfactory cells in our nose are stimulated directly by the molecules present in the odor of the foodstuffs we eat. Saliva is not required for our nose to taste! When we get a cold, our sense of taste is diminished. Our mouth is usually dry, and as a consequence our taste buds operate less effectively with limited saliva. Simultaneously, our nose is usually stuffed and blocks out all odors. This combination makes us unable to smell our food and unable to taste it. It is understandable, then, that wine tasters don't actually taste wine with their taste buds as much as they "taste" the wine's bouquet with their noses.

We've all heard the expression, "You have great taste!" Personal bias aside, can our tongue really taste the same food differently than someone else's tongue? Sure it can, and the taste of the same food can indeed vary under normal conditions for ourselves as well. Genetics and age both play a key role in taste bud function. Infants and senior citizens need strong flavors to awaken their taste buds. The age of our taste buds is significant when it comes to their tasting ability, but for all ages, saliva is the flavor master. Have you ever raved over a meal at a favorite restaurant only to become disappointed with the same meal on a return visit? The truth is, although there are chefs that deserve low marks for consistency, the majority of our disappointments really depend on the changing consistency of our saliva. This fluctuates depending on our mood and how wet or dry our mouth is. A veal picata will taste much different when we are happy and hydrated with our juices flowing than when we are stressed and parched! If you do find yourself down in the dumps and hungry, don't rely on an alcoholic drink to turn your taste buds back on. The alcohol acts as an astringent on your tongue and will only dull your sense of taste even further. The best antidote for repeating a great taste is a great laugh. So while you're reading your menu next time you're dining, tell a good joke for salivation's sake; it will make your food taste much better.

A discussion of taste is incomplete without a brief comment on why so many of us crave the taste of chocolate. While chocolate does have sugar, this is not the main ingredient that spurs on our desire. It is rather several chemical ingredients in chocolate that deliver a one-two punch to our body and make us reach for it during times of emotional upheaval—when we're blue, stressed, passionate, or missing a loved one. Chocolate contains phenylethylamine (PEA), the same chemical released in our brain when we have a romantic rush. Chocolate also has a high carbohydrate load that, when eaten, causes our pancreas to produce more insulin leading to an increase of the neurotransmitter serotonin in our brain. Since serotonin is one of our body's most powerful calming neurotransmitters, the combination of the romance of PEA and the serenity of serotonin, even in low amounts, makes chocolate a truly addictive substance.

TEETH GRINDING

What do a yellow light, a traffic cop, and teeth grinding (bruxism) have in common? Simply put, they all help direct traffic! The road signs are obvious here, but teeth grinding! What's the connection? The answer involves an explanation that certainly would have helped two of the most famous grinders of all time: General George Custer and Cleopatra.

One in seven adults regularly grind their teeth and nearly every child does prior to getting their permanent teeth. For most of us, though, teeth grinding happens in short bursts every day. Periods of anger and determination often provoke it. While speculation and risk-taking events like spending time at the dog races, horse races, or craps table are also instigators, trivia buffs should know that the most common foodstuff or beverage associated with bruxism is alcohol.

We usually grind our teeth while we are asleep or subconsciously while we are awake. In either case, the rhythmic clenching and abrading of our teeth is primarily a way for us to redirect our personal energy or stress "traffic." Unfortunately for George Custer, his stress and love for battle was not totally quenched by nightly grinding. In fact, the opposite was true! Union military history records that General Custer usually set the timing of his battles in relation to the soreness of his mouth. The greater the grinding, the more convinced he was of impending victory. His

theory seemed to work until he came upon his untimely ambush and demise at the Battle of the Little Big Horn, an event that many of his colleagues, including his teeth, had warned him against.

Cleopatra was one of the most famous teeth grinders in ancient times. Her wealth, power, and beauty in Egypt caught the attention of Marc Antony during his courtly visits, but her bruxism during stately business was also quite remarkable. Its interesting that scholars record that Cleopatra gave in to stress by diving into an asp pit and succumbing to the poisonous teeth of one of the snakes.

It's safe to say that few of us will die in battle or from the venom of a snake because we grind our teeth; however, continued bruxism may cause wearing and loosening of our teeth. So if you have a history of bruxism, a bite plate may help lessen the damage of your habit.

In the last decade there has been a great deal of curiosity concerning a condition called Temporomandibular Joint Syndrome. Symptoms of TMJ include headaches, jaw tenderness, and a dull, aching facial pain. The cause of TMJ appears to be related to the incorrect inner workings of the jaw joints and the ligaments that support them. Usually, spasm of the chewing muscles is involved. Although it is correct to say that teeth grinding or teeth clenching may bring about this spasm, TMJ is brought on when there is an underlying compensatory mechanical failure of the joints and supporting ligaments. In other words, we shouldn't principally blame TMJ on teeth grinding.

THIRST

The sensation of thirst is one of the greatest examples of how the body regulates itself. When the body is risking dehydration, the brain will signal an urge so strong it outweighs the drive for food and in most cases the drive for sex.

Water makes up about 70 percent of your body. It is vital to all of your bodily functions. The fluid in your body also contains a balance of salts like sodium, potassium, chloride, magnesium, and calcium. It is often referred to as an electrolyte soup, and it generates the low-voltage electricity that allows nerve cells to transmit signals throughout the body. When you think about it, Dr. Frankenstein may have had a point.

The reason thirst is so important to our existence and balance is that it regulates the amount of water we take in. We need to replenish our water after we sweat or urinate, but too much can cause disaster. In the 1983 Chicago ultramarathon, two runners had to be hospitalized not for dehydration but for virtually drowning themselves. They took in twenty to twenty-four liters of fluid to replace the water they lost through sweat, but did nothing to replace the salt they had lost. The water they drank diluted their body fluid, throwing off their internal balance.

Some of the excess water they guzzled went to the runners' brains, which made them appear to be drunk. They both had to be hospitalized so that their electrolytes could be restored. Athletes who perspire a great deal can drink electrolyte formulas to prevent this from happening.

Even though scraping your tongue off the roof of your mouth with a spatula may be your first clue that you are experiencing severe thirst or dehydration, thirst is not caused by the salivary glands. It is the control center in the brain called the hypothalamus that sends the signals to the salivary glands to stop the secretions so it will produce the sensation of thirst. Thirst is so uncomfortable, it assures that we will respond to it.

When you drink in response to thirst, the brain will be signaled immediately, even though your body hasn't had a chance to absorb the fluid. This is to prevent you from taking in too much fluid at one time. It takes thirty minutes to an hour to fully absorb and distribute the fluid. If the body waited that long to register that the thirst has been quenched, you could potentially burst like an overfull water balloon.

TICKLES

There is nothing more fun than to tickle a baby and watch her squeal with delight. If you are her mother or someone she knows, she will giggle with abandon. However, if you are a stranger, she might just as easily burst into tears even though the sensations to her body will essentially be the same.

Tickling is believed to be caused by an exciting of fine nerve endings beneath the surface of the skin. But psychology plays an important role. A baby sees tickling from her mother as a game. It is like a mock attack she knows will not do her any harm. However, if the "attacker" is someone she doesn't know, she may become frightened. Her instincts will respond to what could be an actual threat.

Tickling isn't only for babies. In fact, the pleasure associated with being tickled is supposed to increase as you age. Just like with babies, if you trust the person who is tickling you, you can let yourself go to the pleasing sensations. You respond with laughter, which has its own pleasures, and will also experience a quickening of the pulse and a raising in blood pressure as the body becomes keyed up and alert.

If you have ever watched children in a tickle fight, you can see how tickling can become torture. Part of the pleasure of tickling is knowing that the tickler will stop when asked. Tell that to an eight-year-old who has brought his younger sister to her knees.

A tickle fight and a tickle match are very different things. Children have shown very scientifically that the response to tickling is one of the few that can be blocked by "mind over matter." The acknowledged rule of a tickle match is to keep from laughing at all costs. But who is actually winning? What children don't realize is that if you will yourself not to laugh, you will block the tickling sensation but may replace it with actual discomfort. The nerve fibers that respond to tickling are the same ones that respond to pain.

Although everyone has their favorite tickle spots, the tickle potential of any given bodily crevice depends more on the skin surface than its actual location. The smoother and hairier the skin, the more it responds to tickles.

This is probably why chimpanzees have been shown to make a chuckling sound similar to laughter when they are tickled.

Tickling can be fun, exciting, and erotic. But, unfortunately, it is something you can't do to yourself. This is probably because half the fun is trying to squirm and wiggle away.

TOUCH

There are heat receptors in your skin, located in the middle dermis layer. If you touch something hot, the receptors will rapidly fire messages to the hypothalamus, which then sends messages through the nervous system for you to take your hand (foot, rump, etc.) off the stove (hot iron, crock pot, curling iron), then jump up and down and yell all kinds of expletives.

If you touch something hot but the heat is not extreme and poses no threat, your heat receptors will eventually adapt to the temperature. This is why a hot bath will feel too hot until you wriggle your body under the water and give the heat receptors time to acclimate.

If something is more than forty-four degrees centigrade, you will feel intense heat, but if you have a bath that is too hot, your body might be fooled into thinking it is too cold. This is because your cold receptors are not activated in temperatures above forty degrees centigrade but will discharge in temperatures over forty-five degrees.

Your cold receptors operate in the same way as the heat receptors. This is why you can wade into a pool up to your navel, but will not want to take the plunge. Unless the pool is icy, your body will acclimate quickly and you will have the sensation that the pool is warmer than the outside air temperature, even if it is considerably cooler.

TREMOR

Just mention the word "tremor" to most Californians and déjà vu visions flash before their eyes. In geology, a tremor signifies the alternating contraction and relaxation of a fault line beneath the surface of the earth. In muscle physiology, a similar physical definition exists, with a comparable emotional gestalt. When we tremble, our voluntary muscles alternate between contraction and relaxation in an involuntary way causing us to experience feelings of anxiety akin to the anticipation of an earthquake. There is another tremor similarity that geology and physiology share. As not all parts of the country are prone to earthquakes, not all parts of our body are equally prone to trembling. Trembling occurs in our body parts that are primarily composed of small muscle groups, such as our hands, feet, jaw, and head. These muscle groups are apt to tremble more often because they contain a greater percentage of red muscle fibers (the type called upon for sprinting rather than long distance running). This anatomical tapestry allows for a greater number of muscle fibers to be chemically triggered into action. Trembling is a result of the oscillating quick bursts of energy that predictably follow.

A commonly held belief is that tremors are precursors to a serious medical problem. The real scoop is that nearly everyone under the age of fifty has a normal identifiable tremor at least once a month. Over the age of fifty, a slight persistent tremor (detectable when we try to perform fine motor skills such as those used in writing a letter) affects nearly one in five people. This annoying symptom is usually unrelated to disease and consistent with our genes and our aging nervous system. Fear, excitement, and moments of extremely heightened emotion are the common causes of a tremor. The chemical messenger in our body that is responsible for the initiation of a tremor is the hormone epinephrine, widely known as adrenaline. Since epinephrine is normally found in our body, a fair question is: What is it about the hormone that causes a tremor to occur? In short, it's quantity. When we are stimulated by external events that awaken our memory of past emotional experiences, epinephrine is released by the adrenal gland in a sudden surge. It's this glandular unloading of epinephrine that directly causes the quiver in our lips and the oscillatory response of our muscles.

Aside from pure emotion, what else can cause tremors? Chances are we're already pretty familiar with the association of alcohol withdrawal and trembling. After drinking a little too much socially, our nerves develop a temporary dependence on the depressant effects of the alcohol. As this depressed or relaxed effect wears off, our body compensates by overstimulating itself, leading to a trembling condition. Fortunately, unlike the headache and hangover, this trembling mechanism rights itself within a matter of hours.

While alcohol is associated with tremor, caffeine usually is not. The reality is that if you drink four to five cups of strong coffee within twelve hours (one in six Americans do), your chance of getting a mild form of caffeine poisoning—agitation, nervousness, and light trembling—is nearly 100 percent. If you're shaking your head in disbelief, try threading the head of a needle after your last cup. I guarantee you'll take another coffee break before you're finished.

Next to alcohol and caffeine, there is at least one other reg-

ular foodstuff that you should associate with heretofore unexplained tremors—sugar. It seems children are prone to tremors
after they eat a meal heavy in sugar (more than three ounces).
Studies have shown that concentrated doses of refined sugar increase adrenaline levels in children. Any parent will confirm that
the usual fallout from an overindulgent pediatric sweet tooth is
agitation and hyperactivity. Few of us have considered the trembling limb as more than an indication of the child being tired. Now
we know the rest of the story.

There are many situations in which a sudden tremor is startling, but few would argue that no one trembling circumstance is
more uncanny then a good scare from a bedtime or nighttime
tremor, called the somnolent, or sleepy lurch. At some time in our
lives, 80 percent of us will experience a bedtime tremor. The more
creative and imaginative our personality is, the more the lurch is
part of our lives.

First, what's happening? A sleepy lurch usually occurs when
we are drowsy or at the point of falling asleep. For some of us the
tremor occurs during a phase of sleep called Rapid Eye Movement
(REM), a period when we have our most vivid dreams. Whether we
are at the point of drowsiness or going through REM sleep, the
cause of the lurch mechanism is the same: Our mind is trying to
catalogue our experiences for the day. Part of this operation involves processing our past day's laughter, fear, and other highly
charged emotional events into memory storage. During this pro-
cedure, the more vivid and specific our recollection (high creativ-
ity/imagination), the more stimulated our body becomes. Our
muscle's normal response generally is a several-second episode of
diminished or total loss of tone (pure relaxation). This moment of
complete relaxation, called cataplexy, is immediately followed by a
compensating surge of adrenaline back to our muscles. Predictably, this contraction and the corresponding jerk of our vulnerable

muscles causes us to awaken frightened and bewildered. This lurching response is sometimes so dramatic and energized that it causes us to knock over objects within our reach such as an alarm clock or a night lamp. Sometimes this muscle contraction is even strong enough to jolt us out of bed.

WHISPERS AND VOCAL CHANGES

When you want to speak so only the person to whom you are speaking will hear you, you may try to whisper. The funny thing is that not everyone knows how. Children sometimes do not know how to whisper. They will make their voices raspy, but they will still be loud. You can only hope that by the time they are grown they will have gotten the hang of it.

When you whisper, you are actually doing everything you would normally do to speak, without the use of your vocal cords. It is the vocal cords that give your voice clarity and clear projection in addition to the other components of speech.

To create speech, the cerebellum in the brain coordinates the movement of the larynx (voicebox) and tongue through nerve signal regulation. Here is the actual process. Speech is made up of vibrated air. The air comes from the lungs and is modulated by the opening and closing of the vocal cords in the larynx. The vocal cords are flaps across the windpipe that can produce sound by vibrating when air passes across them. The sound is made louder by resonating in all the hollow cavities of the throat, nose, and sinuses.

Speech is formed when you breathe out. The airflow through the glottis, which is the slit between the vocal cords, causes the vibration of the vocal cords. This produces the waves of sound.

The tongue, mouth, jaw, and lips will produce certain sounds used in the formation of speech patterns. A v sound is made with a vibration and an f sound is the process without the vibration. To make consonants, the tongue, roof of the mouth, teeth, and lips come into play. Vowel sounds are produced by changes in the shape of the mouth cavity and larynx.

The length and thickness of your vocal cords determines the pitch of your voice. Women have high-pitched voices because they have shorter, thinner vocal cords than men.

When you have an inflammation of the vocal cords, whispering can do more harm than good. You may think you are leaving the vocal cords alone, but you are most likely trying to talk without the benefit of full vocal capacity. A true whisper is a gentle hissing of air without the movement of the vocal cords. With laryngitis, there is no way to determine how much air you are exhaling because you are unable to adequately produce sound. What you have sounds something like Lauren Bacall, which may be sexy, but can cause you many extra days of discomfort.

Have you ever noticed that if you get really upset your voice may start to shake? You might be having a really good argument with your spouse, making good points, and your voice gives way. It is hard to sound effective when your voice sounds like a five-year-old trying to choke back tears. Although you may not really want to cry, your voice is responding to the high emotional stress. The larynx is very susceptible to tension. When you become distressed, your brain sends messages to the nerve endings in your muscle fibers that you are upset but trying to look calm, which sends messages from the nerve impulses to produce the neurotransmitter acetylcholine. This chemical chain reaction will cause the muscles that control the vocal cords and the muscles that hold the larynx in place to contract.

This could arguably be an evolutionary internal protective mechanism to prevent you from saying stupid things you don't mean in a fit of anger. If you find your voice quivering, the best thing to do is to stop speaking and try to relax.

If you find your voice quivering before you have to make a public speech, it could be the same protective mechanism in place. Most likely it is just fear. You should breathe deeply and steadily and slow down your pace. You can always tell that a public speaker is nervous when he begins to sound like Alvin of the Chipmunks.

YAWNING

hile this book was in the planning stage, if I would tell anyone about "funny feelings" they would invariably ask me "why do we yawn?" Yawning is a harmless phenomenon that, although inspiring universal curiosity, has never really inspired serious research.

When you yawn, your mouth opens as wide as it can, unless you inhibit it for appearance's sake. Your chest cavity expands in an exaggerated way, your shoulders rise, and you may even find yourself having a good stretch.

If you have ever had your ears clog in an airplane, you most likely owe gratitude to the yawn. Yawning will unclog "airplane ears" better than chewing gum or steam cups. This is because it equalizes the pressure in the middle ear when the airplane is descending.

If you have ever been with your spouse at a boring obligatory party, you know how a polite yawn can signal your desire to leave. You can then bid retreat with a polite "the baby was up late last night," unless, of course, your hosts know for a fact that your "baby" has just left for college.

Yawning can sometimes be a bit embarrassing like when you are trying to impress your in-laws, a client, or a new date with your sense of culture. It is common to leave an opera, a concert, or a play yawning like you will never stop. If you are deemed a tasteless

nincompoop, you can vehemently protest, explaining, "I am not bored, I am merely having a physiological response to help correct an imbalance of carbon dioxide and oxygen in my blood caused by shallow breathing in a crowded room for the past two hours." They may not be impressed, but at least they will be better informed.

Or you could say that you are simply protecting them like our evolutionary cousins the baboons. Baboons yawn as a warning signal to each other to beware of impending danger. Although there is growing scientific evidence to support this theory, psychologists continue to look for definitive results that link our yawning reflex with our evolutionary precursors.

The best excuse for an inopportune yawn might be "the devil made me do it." In the middle ages people believed the yawn was caused by the devil wanting to possess you. This developed into the ritual of making the sign of the cross over your mouth at the first sign of the devilish yawn. This eventually became a simple pat.

You may as well skip the explanations altogether, gently pat your mouth, and say "excuse me." After all, yawning is involuntary. Although you can consciously make yourself yawn, you cannot consciously stop one from happening.

Yawning is a total reflex that occurs when the nerves in the brain stem find there is too much carbon dioxide, the body's waste gas, in the blood. When you yawn, the muscles in your mouth and throat spasm and force your mouth to open wide to allow the carbon monoxide to escape while your chest cavity expands to allow for a large intake of oxygen-rich air.

In fact, while I have been writing this I have had to make every effort to control the impulse to yawn myself—without success.

It seems yawning is highly susceptible to the power of suggestion, especially if someone yawns in front of you. Oddly enough, however, if a baby or animal yawns, they do not usually cause a chain reaction. Yawning researchers, confounded over why yawns are contagious, suggest that your responsive yawn to another's is an involuntary attempt to return a perceived warning. Children pose no such risk!

Whatever the cause, a yawn is not necessarily an impolite action. It's really the body giving us a status report on the world around us.

ABOUT THE AUTHOR

R. ALAN XENAKIS attended the University of New Hampshire, where he received his Bachelor of Arts degree, before earning a dual doctorate in medicine (M.D.) and science (Sc.D.) from Boston University, and a Masters in Public Health from Harvard University. Intent on a career where he could positively impact the process of public health education, Dr. Xenakis served as medical editor at CBS television's Boston affiliate, WHDH-TV, where he received 13 Emmy Award nominations and one Emmy Award. The American Cancer Society also honored him with its prestigious Sword of Hope Award for excellence in radio health programming. In 1992 Dr. Xenakis won the Freddie Gotbaum Award for excellence in wellness programming. He continues to entertain and educate the public with weekly health radio segments on WHDH radio in Boston. As co-chairman of Health Management International, a national health care communications company, he creates easy-to-understand and fun audio, video, and television programs on health. He is currently working on a syndicated television version of *Why Doesn't My Funny Bone Make Me Laugh?* to air in 1993.

He spends his family moments in North Andover, Massachusetts, with his wife, Elizabeth Stern Xenakis, who is a registered nurse and former actress. On weekends, he coaches soccer and hockey for his son Nicholas and other children.

MEDICAL ALERT!

Are there any medical mysteries you would like explained? Send me your toughest questions, and if you are the first reader to submit a mystery I attempt to solve in the next volume, I'll send you a complimentary copy and acknowledge your contribution in the book.

I'd love to hear from you, so send your letters to:

DR. ALAN XENAKIS
℅ Villard Books
201 East 50th Street
New York, New York 10022